BAXTER

BAXTER
The Party's Over
An Autobiography

Jim Baxter with John Fairgrieve

Stanley Paul
London Melbourne Sydney Auckland Johannesburg

Stanley Paul & Co. Ltd
An imprint of the Hutchinson Publishing Group
17–21 Conway Street, London W1P 6JD

Hutchinson Publishing Group (Australia) Pty Ltd
PO Box 496, 16–22 Church Street, Hawthorne, Melbourne,
Victoria 3122
PO Box 151, Broadway, New South Wales 2007

Hutchinson (NZ) Ltd
32–34 View Road, PO Box 40-086, Glenfield, Auckland 10

Hutchinson Group (SA) Pty Ltd
PO Box 337, Bergvlei 2012, South Africa

First published 1984

© Jim Baxter 1984

Set in Baskerville by BookEns, Saffron Walden, Essex
Printed and bound in Great Britain by Anchor Brendon Ltd,
Tiptree, Essex

ISBN 0 09 158450 7

Contents

Acknowledgements
Foreword
Introduction 1
1 Off to Ibrox 16
2 And put it on the bill, please! 24
3 Celtic – just one more team 30
4 The wonder of Wembley 39
5 Good-night, Vienna 48
6 Transfer truths 54
7 Second-rate Roker 60
8 Down in the Forest 71
9 The homecoming 78
10 The great ones 86
11 Golden Millar 93
12 The world's a stage 98
13 Girls galore 102
14 North American interludes 120
15 Easy come, easier go 134

Photograph Acknowledgements

The authors and publisher would like to thank Colorsport, the *Daily Record* and Sportapics for allowing use of copyright photographs.

This book is dedicated to my children,
to my mother and father,
and Scot Symon, an outstanding football manager
and a true gentleman

Introduction

The title of this book could equally well have been *The Party's over*, for that just about sums up my story. But it was some party while it lasted, and it lasted for a long time. I could bring in a few more songs . . . 'My way', 'No regrets', 'What a swell party it was!' They would all be equally suitable, I suppose.

But if there's one thing I do not want to imply, it's the smallest suggestion of self-pity. If, in the year I write this book, I don't possess a mansion with a swimming-pool, a Rolls in the garage, and a business to pay for it all, the fault is mine. The choice was mine, and knowing myself well enough – I think – there wasn't really any other way.

I know that there are plenty of folk who think I was silly, a fool to myself. They say I should have kept playing for at least five years more than I did. They say all sorts of things, and there is some truth in what they say.

If I had my career all over again, would I still have been as daft? Would I still have chased the birds with such dedication, swallowed the booze with such enthusiasm, gambled away a fortune with such . . . well, nonchalance, shall we say?

I don't know. It's impossible to know such things. It's the difference between the impulsiveness of youth and the wisdom of maturity – even though there are lots of old fools around. Of course, if I could be twenty again and know what I know at forty . . . that would be a different matter altogether, wouldn't it? That's what we'd all like.

INTRODUCTION

In a senior professional football career that lasted about thirteen years, I packed in a lot of living. I played all over the world, from Hong Kong to Vancouver, and I played with and against the best. I played for Raith Rovers, Rangers, Sunderland and Nottingham Forest – and for the Rest of the World against England. For years, I was more or less an automatic choice for Scotland, and I can never forget having been captain of Scotland – the greatest honour of all.

I made a lot of money, I spent a lot of money, and I lost a lot of money. No doubt I made a few enemies, although I honestly can't think of any. I know I made many, many friends – who are still friends.

This book is about what I think and what I have done – in certain cases about the people I have done it with. It is as frank as I can make it, without losing any of my friends.

And if the party *is* over, who is to say there won't be another to come?

There's no other way to look at it, is there? I have been lucky, there can be no doubt about that. I have been lucky, because I was given, by nature, a talent to play football. Nature also gave me other things, like a capacity to enjoy life, and that's equally important.

I can't stand moaners and groaners and hypocrites and scrooges. Surely, it would have been a waste of my football talent if I hadn't enjoyed the good things I became able to buy. If that sounds like self-justification, take no notice. I see no need to justify myself to anybody. Perhaps I did enjoy myself too much, but what's too much? Moderation, as far as I'm concerned, is for moderate people. Half-measures are for little people.

And if I *was* a fool to myself, I was at least my own fool. I always bought my round, too. I always will, or you won't find me in the pub.

Nowadays, I am asked many questions by my friends: what do I really think of so-and-so? What do I really think of many things.

These are questions I never dodge. Why bother? I

have always been fairly honest with myself, I am honest with others.

One question I'm often asked is what do I think of Kenny Dalglish? I can't think of an easier question or a more sincere answer.

Kenny Dalglish is the kind of football player loved not only by the kids but also by the parents and, of course, the fans. He is a model of what a professional footballer *should* be – and I realize, in saying that, that some folk may make invidious comparisons with myself. So let them!

Obviously, I would not want young supporters to see Jim Baxter as a model footballer – not off the field. But Kenny is not only class *on* the field . . . he stays that way, in every circumstance.

We were, we *are*, different. I'm not interested in any argument about who may have been the superior player although, as usual, I have my own opinions. But when you think of the many thousands of pounds Kenny could have made had he moved around more . . . when you think of the countless temptations he must have resisted . . . well, he has my admiration. Without reservation.

Then there's Charlie Nicholas. Charlie has been taking quite a lot of criticism, since he went from Celtic to Arsenal. As far as I'm concerned, Arsenal won the pools when they bought Charlie. Only maybe the cheque is post-dated.

I would bet any kind of cash – so long as I have it – that Charlie will make each and every one of his critics feel silly. He is too good not to be a success, and don't tell me about the greater challenge of English football. If you can play, you can play, and that's all there is to it. In a way, Charlie reminds me of the way I used to be. He has confidence, even arrogance.

But football, to use that weary cliché, is a team game. Is Charlie getting enough help? Is Arsenal the right club for him? Who really knows? My money is still on Charlie – on genuine talent. How else could I think?

INTRODUCTION

Bryan Robson? Well, I've seen Bryan play several times live, and frequently on the box. He has all the subtlety of a rhino, but see how he keeps winning the ball. And if a team isn't in possession of the ball, then it can do nothing – except, possibly, back-track, hoping for the best. Bryan wins the ball, then he uses it well. He is no tanner-ba' player. He is a formidable competitor. He just *might* be approaching the stature of Dave Mackay. He would be in my team, any time.

Glen Hoddle is another player who reminds me of myself, because he can look up and see just about the whole park in an instant. The phrase for what he has is, I think, 'panoramic vision'. Not that this kind of extraordinary eyesight is enough. Once you've seen the situation, you have to do something about it. More than once, I've been on the ball, looked up and around, and then back-heeled to somebody.

Hoddle wouldn't think twice about doing something like that. But I doubt whether he can really accept responsibility. I don't think he can change the way a game is going. If his team is in trouble, then so is he. That's one big difference between Hoddle and Robson. Robson will always clench his teeth and steam in. He is not interested in defeat. That doesn't mean I wouldn't want Hoddle in my team. But, if it's all the same to you, give me Mr Robson right there alongside him.

The other Robson is a somewhat different matter. Bobby Robson, who else?

I've no doubt that he is a very pleasant, gentlemanly kind of person, but, let's be quite frank, such persons are a hundred a penny. They don't achieve anything, that's the trouble.

It's not enough to make many friends, it's not enough to be liked, or even to be respected. What the hell is the good of a manager of England who can't beat Denmark at Wembley. Denmark for God's sake! Butter, blondes, beer, porno shops and the statue of a mermaid. It's crazy!

INTRODUCTION

England has immense football resources, but persists in picking managers who are comfortably part of the establishment, like Walter Winterbottom, Alf Ramsey and Ron Greenwood. In Ramsey's time, the World Cup was won, but, outside England, that was seen as a freak episode in the history of football. This theory has since been proved to be sound, not least by Scotland.

It seems to me there's only one man for the England job. There has been only one man for years, and that is Brian Clough. Now there's a man who would realize that it's 1984, not 1954. There's a man who would change things.

And that, of course, is why he isn't manager of England!

Similarly, Alex Ferguson should be manager of Scotland. Can that be seriously questioned by anybody who believes Scotland should be doing much, much more with its wealth of international talent.

If the SFA had an ounce of imagination, Alex Ferguson, whose Aberdeen side is Britain's best along with Liverpool, would be asked: 'Look, how much are you being paid now? Don't answer that! Just add on ten grand, and the job is yours!'

As I write, Jock Stein is still in charge. With the best will in the world, I cannot understand why. Jock has done a lot but nobody has yet found the secret of defying advancing age. It is time he retired gracefully with dignity and honour.

I'm convinced that the football writers have kept him in his job up to now, and I can only assume that they have done so because they can't think of anybody else. Well, I have already mentioned one alternative. Another is Jim McLean.

Yes indeed, Jock Stein has an exceptional record with Celtic! Since he left Celtic, he has had to rely on excuses – and on 'lessons learned'. How long do we have to learn the lessons? When do we start passing exams?

Are we to say that Jock Stein doesn't have the material,

INTRODUCTION

that he doesn't have the scope? I trust not. He never stops chopping and changing, and he is not always forced to do so.

Frankly, Scotland should be ashamed of her record in these last half-dozen years or so. Where is the pride of the jersey? Consider those who *do* have such pride . . . Wales and Northern Ireland. And these are the countries we now disdain to play. We have the cheek to say they don't matter, as we side with the English in scrapping the Home Internationals.

Anyway, I hope I've set the record straight so far as my opinion of much of present-day football is concerned. If I've caused some argument, let me assure you that I haven't finished. But perhaps I should now be asking myself . . . where do I begin my own story? Unoriginally, I answer . . . at the beginning.

And if I've had an eventful life, so far, I can't say that there was a lot to get excited about at Hill o'Beath, in Fife, where I was born. Home was a miners' row. Everybody in the family was, or had been, down the pit, and when I look back, I think of these days as great times, though I'm not sure why. I mean, there's not really much to enjoy in a pit village, not by the standards of most people anyway. Four in a bed and outside toilets, mince and potatoes the pride of the menu . . . some way, you might say, from the so-called sophistication I was to sample in later years.

Somebody once said to me, yes, but it must have been character-forming. What's that supposed to mean? These are the kind of clowns who embarrass miners by calling them the salt of the earth, that sort of thing. They've never been in a pit village – except maybe to pass through in a hurry, thinking, how quaint! They've never had a Co-op number, they always have dinner in the evening, they drink half-pints and think they're daring, but they feel they should identify with what they like to call the working-classes. There is, to be sure, a sense of togetherness, even clannishness, among miners and mining folk, probably because they know that if they don't help each other, nobody else will. It could be that a mining-village childhood does form character, but if you go down the pit often enough, it also forms black bits on the lungs.

Anyway, I was normal enough to dislike school and to love football. I wasn't a dunce, to be fair to myself, but I wasn't a star pupil either. It was a question of doing just enough to get by, and spending every spare minute kicking a ball.

There were a lot of good players around, but I managed to get in the Hill o' Beath Primary team before very long. We didn't win much, though, and when I went to Beath High, it was really hard to get into the side. Eventually I made it, and I was about fourteen when I won my first medal. I was proud of that medal, as proud as I've been of any honour. It was the Dick Cup competition, the big one for schools in that part of Fife, and the final was at East End Park, home of Dunfermline Athletic. What a genuine thrill that was, just to set foot on a senior ground, and playing into real nets. Now I have to admit that my football style was beginning to take shape then. Why do I say 'admit', as if I were pleading guilty? Well, I was greedy for the ball. If I wasn't on the ball, I felt I wasn't playing. Naturally, this didn't please the other lads in the team. They thought they could play a bit themselves, and they could. So I came in for stick, especially if I'd been shouting for the ball and then shoved away a bad pass.

Did I say they could play a bit? There was one little lad, Hugh Ness was his name, and he was the best player I ever saw in my life. That's a big statement, so I'll make it again. Wherever Hughie is now, he stays in my memory as the best. I think he must have been only fifteen when he went to Raith Rovers. I saw him a couple of years later, and he was beginning to make his mark in the reserves. But he had one giant disadvantage – he hadn't put on any weight or strength in that intervening time. Seventeen going on fourteen, if you know what I mean. In the gym at 5-a-sides, or on a small park, he could turn you inside out. But on a big park, in heavy going – no, in any going – he just couldn't get away from his man, so he had to beat him about half-a-dozen times. I'm not kidding, that's what he *would* do, but, naturally, this took the puff out of him. Raith had to give him a free transfer. When that happened, it was a terrible disappointment to me, but it broke Hugh's heart.

It must have been a bad blow to his father, also, who used to be with him all the time. I'd have hated that, and my dad knew it. He told me later that he had often watched me play from an anonymous part of the crowd, in case I felt inhibited. He's a thoughtful and sensitive man, another reason why I think so much of him. Like my mother, he was determined that I shouldn't go down the pit. I wonder how many mothers and fathers have felt like that . . . and I wonder how many have been able to achieve the ambition?

So when I left school, I became an apprentice cabinet-maker in Dunfermline. It's supposed to be a great thrill, when you take home your first pay-packet. I can't say I was much thrilled by one pound note and eight old pence. Less tax. It must have cost my mother ten bob a week, giving me seven-and-six pocket money, and paying my bus fares. My pals were working in the pit, of course, and earning about a fiver a week. This meant they had about thirty bob pocket money, and I soon became very fed up with that nonsense. After six months, the fine art of cabinet-making and Jim Baxter parted company. My parents gave in, and I started work at Fordel Colliery, on the 'tables', another art, I suppose, in its own way – separating the coal from the stone – and reasonable money.

For about a year, the only football I played was in the local park on a Sunday, when there might be as many as 22-a-side. It didn't do me any harm, though. Well, when you've got to beat twenty-two men, it's not bad practice, is it?

Meanwhile, I was sampling the delights of a 'bevy', usually before the Sunday games. All highly illegal, naturally, as I'm not sure I was sixteen, let alone eighteen, but the older lads used to sneak us something out. My preference was for a bottle of stout, which could hardly be called a real drink, but maybe it was a sop to my conscience.

Maybe, too, it gave me the courage to *try* to beat these twenty-two men, for which I would get well and truly booted. It set a sort of pattern, no doubt, which I was to follow in rather higher spheres later on. But a couple of the lads at the pit-head started a boys' club side, and we beat everything in sight. Then came the big-time, and I am definitely not joking. Everything is relative, they say, and, to me, junior football with Crossgates Primrose was nearly stratospheric.

Crossgates even gave me a signing-on fee. Fifty quid! I held the money in my hand, and I could hardly believe it. I had never even seen so much money in my life. It wasn't a cheque. Hard cash. Used one-pound notes, believe it or not. I felt capable of ransoming somebody, leaving it in a suitcase on a lonely road somewhere. Instead, not knowing anybody who had been kidnapped, I bought my mother a shining new washing-machine, and she loved it. I'm sure it must have been about the first of its kind in that part of Fife.

Now, for the benefit of the uninitiated, let me say something about junior football. For a start, that word 'junior' isn't really accurate. All ages can play, if, that is, they *can* play at all. The juniors are semi-professional and represent a crucial breeding-ground for the senior ranks. Also, former seniors, full-time professionals, were – and still are – often reinstated junior. They are usually much sought after. They may have grown that wee bit too old and too slow for the top grade, but they still have the essential skills and experience. Equally important, they pass on these skills to the youngsters.

The juniors are, moreover, ferociously competitive. Not so much now as they used to be, I suppose, but there's still plenty of local rivalry, and I know of many local derby matches which give referees nightmares.

INTRODUCTION

Another thing about junior football is that if you're underweight and, well, sort of learning, you are put out on the wing – out of the way of the heavy stuff in the middle of the park, where they don't take prisoners and don't even bother to inform next of kin.

So in my first Scottish Junior Cup-tie, I'm playing outside-left, and the opposition is Tranent Juniors. This is an East Lothian club, just on the edge of coal country. It's where Jock Wallace comes from, which may make some sense in view of what I'm about to say. I'm not quite seventeen years old at the time, and I weigh about nine stone, soaking wet. But of course I've got lots of confidence, even if there were some who thought I had too much of that. We're lining up at the start, and I look casually over at the right-back.

It's not that I was a coward, you understand, but there was nothing wrong with my sense of self-preservation. This man was maybe six feet tall, but he looked like a blend of King Kong, Ernest Borgnine and Bobby Shearer. In fact he made Bobby Shearer look like Danny La Rue, and Bobby could handle himself very well. You may say to yourself, ah, but a real player can always make a monkey even out of a gorilla. That's a good theory. It presupposes that you get tackled only when you've got the ball. I've played in dozens and dozens of matches where that theory is nothing better than a poor joke. I've been kicked up in the air when nowhere near the ball, and so have plenty of other folk. It's called teaching a lesson, and I was beginning to learn that lesson as early as sixteen.

Bobby Simpson, my cousin, was playing in that game against Tranent. He had once played for Rangers, and for a couple of the Fife senior teams. I shouted over to him.

'Bobby, what am I supposed to do about this fella? Look at him! He'll kill. For God's sake, keep me out of this. Just concentrate on the other side of the park, all right?'

I don't pretend to remember exactly what happened

during that game, but I do remember having had what the scribes would call a quiet match. If I did get the ball in space, I got shot of it again right away, and then jumped as high as I could.

That's another lesson that has to be learned early. If you don't jump high enough, you're in trouble. Even so, you can jump six feet from a standing start, and there are still lads who'll get you on the way down. Maybe they're sent off, but they walk off, smiling. Usually, they're not sent off, and then they're laughing.

But that's another matter, elaborated on elsewhere in this book. I still enjoyed my time at Crossgates, always learning and, no doubt, improving. I had to be improving, because there were lots of little stories in the local papers about senior clubs watching me. How I loved these stories! Just to see my name in print, in an ordinary match report – a short 50-word report, even – was a tremendous thrill. But to be mentioned as a potential senior pro was something else altogether.

Anyway, the day came. Raith Rovers offered me a trial. The Rovers may not be such a big power in the land these days – a decline common to all of the Fife clubs – but in the 1950s they were something very much to be reckoned with. There was just one problem – apart from the obvious one of performing well in the trial. Would the under-manager at the pit let me off early on the Saturday? That's not as daft a question as it sounds. For one thing, I needed that job. For another, the under-manager, Mick Johnson, was a hard man, a holy terror. In the kind of job he had, softies wouldn't have lasted five minutes. Mick worked hard at not being a softie. After the shift on the Wednesday, I joined the queue waiting to see Mick. I could hear the older miners exchanging swear-words and other assorted insults. This was the time when you made complaints or asked for favours. Mick was not known for listening with a sympathetic ear to either.

In fact, when I look back, I'm fairly sure there were times when he didn't listen at all. So when it was my turn to put a case for what was called an 'early tow' up the pit, Mick was in an even less receptive mood than usual. You had the impression that to ask him for a favour was a bit like patting a crocodile. 'Aye' he said. 'What do *you* want, then?'

You must understand that when he asked that question, he put it slightly more colourfully, but we needn't go into that. I explained that I needed a line to finish at twelve on the Saturday. The line was to give to the fireman, the immediate superior.

'What fur?'

'Well, I've got this trial for Raith Rovers and . . .'

'A trial for Raith Rovers! You! It's a plate of porridge you need.'

He might have been right at that, considering that I still didn't weigh enough to go out in a high wind.

'What's your name?'

'Eh, well, Jim Baxter.'

He leaned back and stared at me again. 'So you're Baxter. Aye, well.'

It was then that I realized that any reputation I was gaining for playing football could come in handy. Mick had actually heard of me. To be honest, I was quite pleased. I realized, too, the grip football can have on a pit community. Mick may have been an under-manager, but he was still a mining man. He gave me my line. He didn't exactly wish me luck, but I suspect he thought about it. It might have made him sound weak, though. The last thing he could afford.

Up the pit, then, at twelve o'clock instead of half-past-one, straight home for a wash, and mince and tatties. There wasn't any of this rubbish about watching what you ate before a match. No roast chicken and salad. You just wired into whatever was out on the table. Nobody had heard of dietitians, not at Raith Rovers anyway.

It didn't seem to do me any harm. That trial was against Rangers reserves, and I think they won. But they were entitled to win. I'm talking about 1957, and I can well remember some of the lads in the Ibrox colours.

INTRODUCTION

Johnny Valentine was in goal, and they had Ralphie Brand, Jimmy Millar and Davie Wilson and Don Kichenbrand.

You remember Don Kichenbrand? If you ever saw him play, you wouldn't forget him. If you played against him – at centre-half, I mean – he was a nightmare. I don't know who labelled him 'The Rhino', but I can tell you that when he charged in on goal, he looked as if only a bazooka would stop him. I'm not saying he was a great footballer. If I did, he'd probably sue me. But he was some asset to his team, if only for the panic he spread amongst his opponents. On that day Don could only get into the Rangers reserves. It will be easily imagined, then, how good I felt when Raith signed me on professional forms immediately after the match.

I didn't give up my job at the pit. I was a part-timer with Raith, and that was worth only £3 a week in the reserves – and I was in the reserves for about six months. Expenses were about five shillings a week, and if Bert Herdman, the manager, could legitimately get away with paying four bob, he didn't hesitate. For the occasional game in the first team,, I'd get £9, which was not bad at all in those days. Down the pit I was earning about £7, so it all added up very nicely.

Also, I was learning, and learning plenty. I thought my education with the juniors had been fairly stimulating, but when you turn senior professional, it's like going to a football university. The difference is vast. Another thing, I had the best of teachers – or lecturers if you like. Raith had some team, then.

The League side had Charlie Drummond in goal. The full-backs were Willie Polland and Ian Bain. Any Raith supporter worthy of the name will recall the half-back line of Young, McNaught and Leigh. Jimmy McEwan, who went to Aston Villa but who was never given the recognition he deserved, was on the right wing, Bernie Kelly at inside-right, Ernie Copeland at centre-forward, myself at inside-left, and Johnny Urqhuart on the left. That was a team that could easily have held its own in the

INTRODUCTION

Premier League today. It might, in fact, have won the Premier League, but for one thing. Only Willie Polland and I were under thirty. Willie McNaught, that wonderful player, must have been pensionable – an exaggeration, but not much.

Anyway, I was well protected, playing with so many veterans of real class, and I'll always be grateful to them. I progressed so well that I began to give serious thought to going full-time, not a step to be taken lightly. Don't forget, I'd be giving up £7 a week, courtesy of the National Coal Board.

After a few months of being reasonably sure that my name would be up on the first-team lines, I did make the decision. My mother wasn't delighted, but she did appreciate that it was my career – and I impressed on her that, with full-time training, I could surely make the grade permanently.

There was something else she appreciated. Nobody likes going down the pit. Nobody gets up in the morning full of enthusiasm at the prospect of another shift. My job certainly wasn't the hardest at Fordel, but it was a long, long way from giving job satisfaction. A man becomes a miner partly through tradition, and partly because it's often the only job going. There is never any other reason that makes sense. Whenever I hear the comfortably-off talk about miners with mortgages and motorcars, as if they were just like superior bank clerks who happened to get their hands dirty, I feel like asking a few questions. Like . . . Why don't you try it yourself, some time?

Anyway, I suppose I must have been developing new signs of a swollen head. And it must have been noticed . . . The local papers, even the Edinburgh evenings, had been running stories about Jim Baxter being in line for an Under-23 cap. Not stories calculated to restore my modesty. Very shortly before I made up my mind to go full-time, I was at Starks Park, ready to dash off in time for the back-shift . . . two in the afternoon until ten at night. Then out came the secretary.

INTRODUCTION

'Somebody on the phone for you,' she said.

Now there was an everyday kind of message, if ever there was one. But not for me. I don't think I'd ever used the telephone before. I began twittering with nerves, and the secretary didn't make me feel any better when she said that it was a sports writer on the *Edinburgh Evening News* at the other end of the line. He introduced himself, and talked at some length about some special information he had. It seemed I was odds-on to be chosen for Under-23 Scotland against Wales, and would I please wait right where I was, until they came over for an interview. They'd buy me lunch, naturally.

'But I can't,' I said. 'I'm on the back-shift, and I'm starting at two.'

'Forget that,' said this lad. 'We'll pay your shift, and a bit extra. Hang on. See you at two o'clock.'

Two o'clock came and went. So did three o'clock. So did my hopes of a nice forty quid or so, just for talking to a journalist. What was going on here? I was a good-natured sort of bloke in those days – I hope I still am. I didn't lose my head when I discovered that the phone call had been made from the Press box by Andy Leigh and Willie McNaught. Mind you, I could always forgive Willie McNaught anything. He gave me the best advice I ever had. Or, at least, the best advice I ever had – and *took*!

1
Off to Ibrox

We were training at Beveridge Park, a little ground near the main stadium at Starks Park, when Bert Herdman called me over. 'Right, Jim,' he said, just like that, 'it seems Rangers are interested in you. We're going to Ibrox, to see what they have to say.'

Well, I'd been at Raith for nearly three years by this time, and I was happy enough. The money was all right, the other players were mates, and I was always reading my name in the papers. For somebody still in his teens, that wasn't a bad life. Yet somehow, at the back of my mind, there was always the thought that I was really marking time, that a lot lay ahead of me, and it wouldn't be at Kirkcaldy either. And so, in a way, I wasn't flabbergasted when Bert Herdman gave me the news about Rangers. I don't mean I had been expecting it. It was more a feeling that things were taking shape, and that maybe there wasn't much I could do about it.

At the same time, I had doubts – or thought I had, which may or may not be the same thing. For a start, Rangers were not my favourite team. Oh no, my idols as a kid were at Easter Road, where Hibs had some of the greatest of them all, including, of course, Gordon Smith. I remember the thrill of watching that wonderful Hibs side in its infancy – I paid special attention to wee Bobby Combe. I was also a touch anxious. After all, I did have so many good friends at Raith Rovers, and Ibrox was the unknown. Which was how Willie McNaught came to play his part.

Bert Herdman gave me a few hours to get ready for the journey to Glasgow and, in between times, I had a chat with Willie. 'What do you think of this, then?' I said. 'Rangers are after me'.

I remember how his eyes lit up, and I know now how pleased he was for me. 'Jim,' he said, 'I've only one bit of advice for you. Don't hesitate. Sign! Don't quibble, don't haggle. Just accept whatever is on offer. And don't worry about losing your mates here. You won't lose them, even if you're playing against us, and you'll make lots of new ones. All football clubs are basically the same, and the lads think the same way no matter where you go.'

He was right. Willie McNaught was usually right. I signed on the traditional dotted line, Rangers handed over a cheque to Raith for about £27,000, and I was there. At least, I was almost there. For various reasons the actual transfer was not disclosed for three months – and I kept on playing for Raith Rovers. Don't ask me why all this was done. It was away over my head. But it did emphasize how Rangers could keep a secret. It didn't give Bert Herdman a reputation as a blabber-mouth, either.

Ironically, I had hardly stepped inside the door at Ibrox – in July 1960 – when the British Army knocked at my own door. That's how I became one of the very last of the conscripts, and in the Black Watch no less.

Now a lot of people will tell you that conscription and the Army was a marvellous experience, something not to be missed, makes a man of you, all that sort of bull. Personally, I found it was almost a total waste of time. When it comes to pulling strings with the establishment, Rangers are past masters, and I found myself stationed more or less permanently in Central Scotland, at Perth or at Stirling. I think I must have missed one game for Rangers during my Army service, so it wasn't really a time of horrible hardship. What I did learn about the Army, though, was the fact that you couldn't mess them about (not forgetting that every rule has its exception, which I'll explain later). If they said, 'Back by eight,' you were back by eight, and they weren't talking about a minute past eight. At least it was one short period in my life when I had to do what I was told – most of the time.

Yes, and I did my bit for the Scottish tourist industry. One Sunday I was on guard at Stirling Castle, four hours on, eight hours off, over the twenty-four hours. It so happened that two busloads of trippers turned up from Glasgow while I was playing cards with a couple of mates. I can well imagine now what the punters were saying when the buses arrived in the castle courtyard. 'Here, isn't this where Jim Baxter is stationed!.' If you think that sounds big-headed, I should say that the newspapers kept people informed about my movements – within reason.

There we were, happily playing pontoon, nicely relaxed, when an officer strides in. 'Right, Baxter, full dress, there's some visitors want to be photographed with you.' There was no point in arguing and, to be absolutely honest, I did feel slightly flattered. The only trouble was that, it being Sunday, I had to wear No. 1 dress, kilt and all. Let me tell you, I felt a right twit, posing like something outside Buckingham Palace. My legs may have been all right for playing football, but I've never kidded myself that I would have been much good on a Black Watch recruiting poster.

However, the Army did have its compensations and there was one very special one. In the noble cause of showing the flag, the Army sent a team of professional footballers – all conscripts, of course – on a seven-week tour of the Far East. I had never known anything like it, and it has not been equalled, in my experience, since. Hong Kong, Singapore, Saigon, Kuala Lumpur, exotic places straight from the pages of adventure fiction – and, nowadays, from the most expensive holiday brochures. And don't imagine for a moment that we were staying in Army huts. Nothing like that for Baxter and his mates. Certainly not. This was five-star-hotel stuff all the way, and, being professionals against virtual amateurs, we strolled through every game. Exhibition performances, more or less.

At the start of the tour Colonel Gerry Mitchell, a marvellous old man, took us aside and explained to us that we were going out on a high note, as the last of the footballing conscripts. Then he took me even further aside:

'Look, Baxter,' he said to me, 'you heard me tell everybody that all the basic things were paid for by the Army – that's the taxpayer, don't forget. You heard me say that anybody who wanted to go à la carte would have to pay for himself. Same with drinks. I don't want any bills. The trouble is, Baxter, I've got a strong suspicion you won't take a blind bit of notice. I'm just guaranteed to get bills with your name on them, isn't that right?'

'No, Sir,' I said. 'Of course not, Sir. Not me, Sir.' Well, in fact, I went very easy on the extras, more out of respect for the colonel than anything else. It was quite enlightening, all the same, to realize that my reputation at Ibrox – I'd been there for a couple of years at the time – was no secret from the Army authorities.

Another unforgettable memory of that tour is when I met Rita Hayworth, one of the loveliest women I've ever seen, in Kuala Lumpur. That is, when I say I met her, I *almost* met her. She was sitting so close to me in a club that I could have reached out and touched her. I didn't reach out, not because I had suddenly fallen victim to an attack of shyness, but because she was with a lad who looked like an especially ill-natured gorilla. We found out later that he was married to Bette Davis. He should have been ashamed of himself, trying to get off with Rita. Some small consolation came when we persuaded the band to play 'The lady is a tramp' from her film, a big hit that year. She took it well enough, but he looked ready to explode and wipe the floor with all of us. It didn't help when we joined in with the lyrics.

The Far East was surely an episode worth a permanent place in the memory, but the serious business went on at Ibrox. Obviously, I had a lot of contact with James

Scotland Symon, otherwise known as Scot Symon, the finest manager Rangers ever had. He was, and is, a true gentleman . . . with dignity, style and a lot more than a mere touch of class. He epitomized Rangers. He *was* Rangers!

There's no doubt in my mind that he loved the club more than did any fan, and he did so much for the club.. And what did they do to him in the end? They fired him, at a time when Rangers were actually at the top of the League. That must be some sort of record, though not one to be envied. I was with Sunderland when I read the news that he had been fired – it was in the late autumn of 1967. I couldn't believe it. Rangers have won a trophy or two since then, but I can't help feeling that their decline may have started with their treatment of such a wonderful servant. Put it this way: if his class characterized Rangers then, it doesn't now.

Not that I would ever pretend that Scot Symon was liked by everybody. He had his share of enemies – or, at any rate, of those who couldn't stand the sight of him. This was because he had no interest in popularity contests, and that attitude did not exclude the Press. Scot could probably be called one of the old school of managers, who didn't know anything about public relations, but who did know how to manage a great football club. You wouldn't see him in a track-suit, any more than you would see the manager of a big bank come out to the counter and cash cheques for the punters.

He wasn't much of a tactician, granted. But he didn't pretend to be, either. The game is infested now by managers who think they know all about how the game should be played, and who try to impose their daft opinions on people who *can* play. Scot Symon never did make that kind of mistake.

He always stressed that football is a simple game (and so it is, if you're any good at it). An Ibrox team talk would go something like this:

'Now look, always remember that there's no need for fancy stuff, no need to take silly chances. You lads at the back, when you get the ball, just give it to Jim or Ian [McMillan], and they'll take it from there. Your job's done.'

And that's the way it usually worked. Scot Symon knew a player when he saw one, too, and nobody can tell me that the Rangers team in the early 1960s wasn't among the best in the club's history. Perhaps *the* best.

Some would say that Rangers were lucky to have ball-players like McMillan and me playing at the same time for the same team, and I'm not going to argue too much about that. But there was an awful lot more to it than beating a man, or passing a ball to where it could cause the most damage. The men who won the ball, men like big Harold Davis, Bobby Shearer and Eric Caldow, they were absolute professionals, always right on top of their jobs. Then there was Jimmy Millar at centre, a fantastic player, and I'm not exaggerating. Jimmy could take a pass, shield the ball for ages, then do just the right thing with it. Often enough, the right thing was a shot into the back of the net. Jimmy was brainy, too, and he worked perfectly with Ralphie Brand, one of the most dangerous goal-scorers in the business. I couldn't count the number of times I've lifted a ball over a defender's head, knowing – *knowing* without a doubt – that Ralphie would be on to it like a cobra.

When you bear in mind that we also had a couple of wingers who could not only run like deer, but who could also score, well, it wasn't a bad side at all. Did I say two wingers? Here's me underestimating again. Apart from Davie Wilson on the left – Davie would get about 30 goals a season – there was Alex Scott, a real flyer, and he was followed, of course, by wee Willie Henderson. If you were playing in the middle of the park for Rangers in these days, you certainly had plenty of options on what to do with the ball when you got it.

These were easily the best five years of my life. The most successful, the most enjoyable, if maybe not the most profitable from a financial viewpoint.

Let's look at that last item first. Finance. Well, when I

joined Rangers in 1960, my basic was £22 a week. When I left for Sunderland in 1965, that figure had soared to all of £45 a week. Now it is only too accurate to say that there were many thousands of folk who would have been delighted with that sort of money. But there were *not* many thousands of folk playing for Rangers and drawing in very big crowds of paying customers every week.

We were paid bonuses. Some bonuses! The League allowed £3 for a win, and we usually copped that. Not such a big deal, though, was it? Then, at Christmas and at the end of the season, we were paid extra lump sums, depending on what we had won, over the piece. These lump sums seldom came to more than £1,500 a time, less tax. So we're probably talking about an annual wage (which relied heavily on winning nearly everything in sight) of under £4,000).

I didn't like that one little bit, and I didn't hesitate to make my feelings generally known – and known specifically to the manager. This sort of behaviour was practically unheard of. By tradition it was the responsibility of the captain to transmit any dressing-room grievances to the boardroom, but wee Bobby Shearer wasn't interested in the responsibility. Bobby was a great Ranger. He would have played for nothing, I'm sure. So he wouldn't protest on our behalf. 'Well, Bobby,' I'd say to him, 'if you won't go upstairs, I will.'

And I did. Bobby never appreciated that, and he's a man I'd never willingly offend. I was very fond of him, and still am. But all the loyalty and gung-ho stuff, while sounding good, didn't pay the rent.

It has to be said that Rangers have a poor record when it comes to standing by their players and looking after them. All right, so you do your job, and you're paid your money, but you'd think there might be a bit more to it than that . . . when the time comes to go. Not at Ibrox, there isn't. When you're no longer any use, off you go. No sympathy. Perhaps there have been exceptions. I see Willie Waddell is still welcome at Ibrox, and no doubt big John Greig got a good pay-off (but that would have been a matter of contract, anyway, wouldn't it?). How many more? In these circumstances, I don't blame myself for some of the liberties I took with Rangers.

2

And put it on the bill, please!

You hear all sorts of tales about players who mess their clubs about, who are always in the headlines. Such tales were often told about me, and I'm not denying them. Not all of them, anyway. In a way, I did mess Rangers about. I suppose I did some incredible things. I tell myself now that I must have been out of my mind. And then again, did I do any real harm?

The truth is that any star – and I *was* a star by this time – can get away with murder. On one condition – he has to balance it all up as soon as he steps out onto that football park. Directors and managers will usually look upon a player's off-the-field antics with a certain fatherly indulgence – *if* that player is attracting the crowds and helping to win matches. There's no doubt in my mind that I did bring the punters in, and that I did help to win matches. Otherwise, Rangers would have got rid of me in double-quick time.

One of my favourite stamping grounds was the St. Enoch Hotel, right in the middle of Argyll Street. That place has many a happy memory for me. I didn't find it too expensive, either. Well, the Rangers board used to meet there for its weekly get-togethers, and I suspect the directors didn't stint themselves, either. They would just sign the bill. So did I.

My appetite for the high life was first whetted when we began winning trophies and championships. In my five years at Ibrox we won four League Cups, three Championships and three Scottish Cups. By tradition, after each triumph, we would appear on the balcony of the St. Enoch Hotel to show the cup to the crowds below. Then it was down to the residents' lounge, and right through the card. Some of the other players – correction, most of the other players – seemed a bit shy, at first, about enjoying themselves at the club's expense. Even after a Cup Final victory! It was an attitude I could never understand.

Who were the crowds down there in Argyll Street cheering? Who did they want to see? Who would they come back to Ibrox to see, at the first available opportunity? The directors? The manager? Some chance! As far as I was concerned, we had done the business, and the sky was the limit. If we didn't get a suitable remuneration in our wage packets, we could surely find compensation from the stock of luxuries at the St. Enoch Hotel.

But quite soon I grew tired of waiting until a Cup Final before enjoying a not-so-quiet celebration. The boss of the hotel's function facilities was a great friend of mine. We shared an affection for horse-racing on TV and, after training, I would often give him a call:

'Busy today?'

'No, no, Jim, come on over.'

Comfortably ensconced in front of the TV set, with a handy line to the bookmaker, we would have a pleasant afternoon, with champagne, smoked salmon sandwiches and the like whenever we had a winner and frequently when we hadn't. Naturally, I arranged for the bill to be sent to Ibrox. On other occasions I would have my friends along for the evening, ordering up anything they fancied. If they wanted to stay the night at the St. Enoch, that was all right, too, and if they fancied a double room, they wouldn't find Jim Baxter narrow-minded.

Naturally, I was getting at least my own share, and in all that time there was never so much as a word said by Rangers, whatever the bill. The other players at Ibrox knew what I was up to, and I suppose there must have been some chat in the dressing-room about me, but I couldn't have cared less about that. They were terrified to do anything out of order. As I say, it was a feat to persuade them to break out after they had won yet another title or trophy. But well, that was their problem. It certainly wasn't mine.

Training was, however, something of a problem for me. Not that I didn't train hard enough, at times. You can't be a professional footballer and get through 90 minutes unless you're reasonably fit. I was lucky in so far as my style of play didn't involve charging all over the park and knocking my pan in, so to speak, but I didn't have a lot of fat to carry, either. The nickname 'Slim Jim' was very much in vogue, and it must have been a boon for the lads who write the newspaper headlines. Not that I objected. But some of the training was really a waste of time, and I could never understand why we were required to train on the morning after a mid-week game. My disinclination to train at all on such mornings caused a few complications, though, to be honest, Thursday morning wasn't the only morning that found me determined to take things very easily.

Davie Kinnear was the Ibrox trainer, and clashes and quarrels were inevitable. I don't think we would have been buddies, even if I had been dedicated to training. We didn't like each other. It was really as simple as that. He thought I was trying to take advantage of him, which was not true. I was merely trying to mind my own business, and I didn't want to be bothered by him. It might have been slightly different, if I had had genuine respect for his training methods. I had none. I'm not saying I was right, and Davie Kinnear wrong. I'm just stating an opinion honestly held then, and still unaltered.

So Thursday morning was definitely the morning after the night before, and it had usually been quite a night. I'd probably been up all night – till about 7 a.m. anyway – or else in bed all night and not sleeping. Whatever the case, I'd be in no mood for running around Ibrox at half-past-ten in the morning. All I needed was a nice, warm bath, and maybe a wee snooze. Essentially, to be

left in peace. So Davie Kinnear would come in, after I had had a bath:
'Done any training?'
'Sure, I have, what do you think?'
'Why is the gear untouched, then? You're at it.'
'At what? Ach, away ye go.'
'I'm telling the boss.'
'So tell the boss, then. Big deal.'

The rest of the scenario was fairly well scripted, and didn't vary too much. Davie Kinnear would storm out and, after I had dressed, the wee doorman would bring a message from Scot Symon, who wished to see me, please. It was something of a ritual. Up the famous marble staircase I would go. I got to know it well enough not to be overawed by it – although the same could not be said of the other players. Scot Symon would be sitting behind that big desk, a sad look on his face.

'Jim, have you trained today?'
'Aye, of course.'
'Jim, I'm going to ask you again, and I want you to think before you answer. Did you train today?'
'Aw, boss, my stomach's killing me. Besides, did I no' run about enough last night.'
'Jim, Jim, can you not just train a wee bit, to keep Davie happy? He thinks you're overruling him, and we can't have that, can we?'

I saw no reason why not, but I could hardly say as much. Eventually, Scot Symon would say what he always said:

'Oh, Jim, you're an awful boy. Look, just see if you can train a little. It's to keep Davie happy. It's not much to ask, surely.' The matter would rest – until the next time. But training was only one of the areas over which I disagreed with Davie Kinnear.

Being a bachelor, and inclined to stay overnight in Glasgow instead of going back home to Fife, for reasons mostly connected with wine, women and song, laundry started off as a problem. Not for long, however. It was solved by Maggie, a lovely wee person who washed the

Rangers strips. She must have been at Ibrox for a hundred years, and she took an instant liking to me. I would bring in my shirts, socks, etc., and she would give me them back a few hours later, sparkling clean, impeccably ironed. Now and again I'd bring her some cigarettes or chocolates. It was a fine relationship, and did nobody any harm.

Unfortunately, Davie Kinnear adopted a different attitude. I don't know why. Maybe he thought it was one more liberty being taken by that lazy big-head, Baxter. Maybe he also thought it was a chance to put Baxter in his place. I can remember very well the conversation when he confronted me:

'What's this I hear? You've got your personal laundry-maid, is that right?'

'Och no, it's just Maggie doing me a wee favour.'

'Well, it's not on. She's here to work for the Rangers Football Club, and not for you'.

'Does it bother you? Is it getting up your nose?.'

And so on. But that was another fight which Davie Kinnear didn't win. It was a pity he felt he had to start the fight in the first place, though. No wonder we didn't seek out each other's company for a drink and a chat!

To be frank, I didn't have many friends at Ibrox, in a social sense. Most of the other players were married, and didn't feel like joining me for nights on the town. Then there was 'The Clique' . . .

This clique was very much in evidence when I first went to Ibrox, and its members were Sammy Baird, Alex Scott, Eric Caldow and George Niven. They were senior players and as thick as thieves. They took it for granted that they should get most of the privileges, and generally liked to boss the younger players around. This was especially true of Sammy Baird, who was not, I'm afraid, one of my favourite people. On the other hand, I don't suppose I'm top of the pops with him, either, so we're even.

One day Sammy had his come-uppance – something which failed to cause distress among the youngsters. The clique was in the habit of playing head-tennis every day, in the indoor training-area, and we were happy to let them get on with it. At least they were out of our hair. Then the powers-that-be decided that the training-area needed a coat of paint. Whereupon Messrs Baird, Scott, Caldow and Niven strolled through to the small gym which was equipped for badminton.

There was one snag – the gym was already occupied by four of the young players busily engaged in their own version of head-tennis. It *should* have been a snag, shall we say. Sammy didn't see it as such. He ordered the kids out, and they went. I wasn't among those told to get the hell out of it, but I'm not sure my reaction would have been any different. Sammy Baird was a big fellow. I wouldn't bet on it, but I think he was bigger even than Harold Davis. But was he tougher? That I *would* bet against and I'd give odds.

Harry had been a paratrooper, and I'm surprised he bothered to use a parachute. On the football park, opponents bounced off Harry, although that's not to say he couldn't play the game. When he tackled, he seldom missed, and he was a better passer of the ball than he was usually given credit for. Harry heard about the way the clique had arbitrarily taken over the gym. He told two of the youngsters, Jim Forrest and Alex Willoughby, that he would join them for a shot at the head-tennis.

Everything went as planned. Forrest and Willoughby were in the gym early, with a couple of others. Big Harry stayed discreetly in the background. Right on cue, Sammy Baird and his mates barged in:

'Right, you lot, cheerio. We're playing here today.'

Harry moved into the centre of the stage.

'Oh, is that right, Sammy. *You're* playing here today, are you? Oh, I don't think so, Sammy. You see, *I'm* playing here. Have you got any objections?'

It has to be recorded that Sammy Baird had no serious objections whatever, and nor did his three fellow-members of the clique . . . which was never quite the same again.

3

Celtic – just one more team

The era of Rangers' supremacy really started in the early 1960s, and, as I've said, I have no doubt that it was among the best sides in the club's history. There may be arguments about one thing only: could we have beaten the great Celtic side shaped and master-minded a few years later by Jock Stein?

Yes, we would have won. I think we would have beaten them four times out of five, and I am well aware that this is no small statement. Ian McMillan and I would surely have been the equal of Bobby Murdoch and Bertie Auld, we would have been at least as solid at the back, and superior in the attack. In saying that about relative forward strengths, I'm not forgetting wee Jimmy Johnstone, a tremendous player.

But to be very honest – honest, I stress, not insulting – when we were winning everything in sight, we didn't take Celtic any more seriously than we took any other side. At that time they just weren't in the same class, and among the many compliments I was paid, I will always cherish what Jock Stein, then at Dunfermline, said:

'Jim Baxter is not playing the Rangers way. Rangers are playing the Jim Baxter way.'

I have to say that this was true. Rangers had always had a reputation for strength and power rather than skill. Not that they lacked a quota of skill. They did have Alan Morton, after all. But those other attributes came first. Without them, you had to be a genius if you wanted to play for Rangers, and even then you weren't sure to get a game. I'm happy to accept Jock Stein's opinion that I changed that attitude, although only temporarily. We did play smooth football, the kind of stuff the purists rave about. I'm not saying that Bobby Shearer and Harold Davis were characterized by elegance, but you must have *some* power, and they had a fair measure of ability anyway.

It was in 1962 that I started my own personal medal campaign, in the Scottish Cup Final against St. Mirren. If I remember correctly, that was the year St. Mirren surprisingly beat Celtic in the semi-final – to the considerable irritation of a number of Celtic fans who tried to break in and stop the game.

Apart from myself, there were three others who were inexperienced in the art of medal-winning. They were Ronnie McKinnon, Willie Henderson and Ralph Brand. This lack of experience was soon to be adjusted. Ronnie, who came in as a last-minute choice, was a bit of a sleepy-head, but he never let Rangers down, and I suppose the only Ranger who didn't play up to form that Cup Final day was that fine centre, Jimmy Millar. But I know why. It also happened that Jim Clunie, the St. Mirren centre-half, had a blinder. In a way, I was pleased to see how Jim was playing because he was a mate of mine, but obviously I would have been a lot less pleased if Rangers had been in any trouble.

We weren't. And as one who was always fond of reading nice things about himself – what player isn't – I recall what the famous 'Rex' of the *Sunday Mail* wrote:

> The game belonged to Baxter more than anyone. He moved all over that field with the polite affability of a young curate looking up his parishioners, and patting a head genially here and there.
>
> If his mates were in trouble, he got them out of it. If the enemy were in trouble, invariably he had got them into it. . . . Any hope St. Mirren may have had was submerged by the shadow of the finest footballer Scotland has seen for many a day – bean-pole Jim Baxter, the next-best Kirkcaldy export after linoleum.

Well, why blow your own trumpet, if there's somebody willing to do it for you? All the same, I couldn't help wondering at the time why Rex had this thing about linoleum. More seriously, I did enjoy the praise, especially when I knew I'd earned it. And whatever they say about the English Cup Final, the Scottish version is far more a celebration of football than you will ever find at the Wembley one, where the grandstands are full of people who wouldn't know the score if they couldn't see it lit up on the big board.

I will have a lot more to say about Wembley later on, in a different context, but we'll stay at Hampden for a moment – and the Cup Final the following year (1963), this time against Celtic.

Now this is probably as good a time as any to mention that delicate subject religion, and to get it out of the way. Why should I mention it at all, you may ask. Why not? Everybody else seems to have an opinion, and I think I'm as well qualified to express a view as anyone.

It is well-known now, of course, that Rangers have a policy of not employing Roman Catholics. They have made several public statements about this and it's hard to work out whether they admit to that policy or not. We are non-sectarian, they say. We will employ anybody, if good enough, they say. Well, that's what they say. Maybe as you read this the first Catholic will have been signed knowingly by Rangers, it being just a co-incidence that none has been found good enough for a very long time.

But I doubt it. And I'll tell you something else. I'm not much bothered one way or the other. If Rangers, as a business concern, want to have a specific employment policy, that's up to them. Protestantism is the official religion, and Rangers are a Protestant club. Nobody else has to like it. Who is really being hurt by it? It could be said – it *has* been said, frequently – that only Rangers are, in fact, hurt. This is because their scouts are prohibited from considering a substantial proportion of promising youngsters. The proportion may be as much as a third in

CELTIC – JUST ONE MORE TEAM

the West of Scotland. Yet if Rangers are prepared to put up with this self-imposed restriction, so what? Again, it's their business.

Is it, then, encouragement of bigotry? That's a tricky question, because the traditional Rangers attitude links them with some nasty chants and songs. But you find bigots in all walks of life, and they're not all religious bigots, by any means. Bigotry is based on ignorance which is not exactly confined to a tiny minority, either. How many bigots, I wonder, are there in the House of Commons, at Royal Ascot, Henley – as well as in Brixton, Bradford and the poorer areas of Glasgow? Plenty!

I don't believe for a minute that a sudden relaxation of the Ibrox policy would have the slightest effect on the bigots of either side. It might even make things worse. There is a good case for saying that the Rangers–Celtic rivalry, religion-orientated or not, is a comparatively harmless medium for channelling bigotry. It could give a certain release. I'm certainly not suggesting that the situation is ideal, but it's a sight better than what happens in Northern Ireland. In the end it's all about education, not necessarily all-religion schools, but the quality of education itself.

Another point worth remembering. Celtic persist in emphasizing that *they* have no religious prejudice against signing Protestants. That's a red herring, if ever there was one. Not a very honest one, either. I admit that in the Celtic side which won the European Cup there were four Protestants – Simpson, Gemmell, Wallace and Auld. Not forgetting the manager, Jock Stein himself! But how many directors of Celtic have been Protestants? So far as I know, none. I believe Stein was offered some sort of seat on the board, but in the demeaning capacity of selling raffle-tickets, more or less.

Anyway, it does not make football or commercial sense for Celtic to confine their players to Catholics. There aren't enough Catholics to choose from, in the first place. If there were, don't you think Celtic would be tempted to ignore Protestants? As it is, they're not daft.

They sign Protestants because they have no real choice – and then they make a virtue of it.

Personally, I was brought up in the Church of Scotland, although this is one part of my upbringing which has not had much impact on me, I'm afraid. If what I have written here lays me open to a charge of bigotry, that's just too bad. As long as I know, in myself, that the charge is false, that's all that matters. As witnesses to my lack of bigotry, perhaps I could call on, oh, say Billy McNeill, Paddy Crerand, Jimmy Johnstone. And a good few more, all of whom go to Mass regularly.

So let's get back to football. To the Cup Final of 1963, against Celtic. The first game was a 1–1 draw. But the score-line should have read: Rangers 1, Frank Haffey 1. Yes, the same Frank Haffey who had played for Scotland in that terrible 9–3 thrashing two years previously. Frank was immense, and it is a great shame that he is still remembered more for Wembley than for Hampden. But in the replay he would have needed the help of a boarded-up goal to save his team. It was no contest. Billy McNeill, I remember, had a fine game for Celtic, but the rest didn't count. Bobby Murdoch, Stevie Chalmers and 'Yogi' Hughes were in the Celtic line-up, but they were nowhere near the calibre and status they were to achieve in the later 1960s ... by which time I was long gone from Ibrox.

Our 3–0 win equalled Celtic's own record of 17 Scottish Cup victories, but that's just one more statistic. That particular Final will surely always be memorable for the fact that many Celtic fans gave up in disgust and went home *at half-time*! Mind you, I can't find it in my heart to fault them – or their capacity for prophecy. The game couldn't have been more than five minutes old when it became obvious that Rangers were going to walk it. It wasn't so much the goal as the way it was scored. Jimmy Millar gave a superb pass to wee Willie Henderson out on the wing. Nobody was marking Willie, so he said 'Thank you very much', ran in on goal, and, as the Celtic defence panicked, crossed to Ralph Brand who was also, incredibly, unmarked. Ralphie didn't miss that sort of chance. A simple goal, a classic goal, but above all a goal that showed how vulnerable the Celtic defence was, despite McNeill.

Meanwhile, I was having an enjoyable game too, and so was big John Greig in the No. 4 shirt. I remember how John received a kick in the face midway through the first half, and how, after a routine wipe with the sponge, he just shook his head and powered on as if nothing had happened. That was typical of Greig!

Davie Wilson got the second just on half-time, thereby sickening the Celtic fans, who were even fighting among themselves, having nothing else to get excited about. When Brand scored with about a quarter of an hour to go with a casual shot which Haffey, I'm sorry to say, should have saved, it was all over.

That's when I began to keep a careful eye on the ball. Through a special sense of dedication, maybe? Well, not exactly. I had my own ideas about what to do with that ball, and they had little in common with my usual ideas, which were to embarrass the opposition. The result was an incident of the variety usually called controversial.

You can always tell when the final few minutes of a match have arrived. Fans of the winning team are whistling, anxious to savour official triumph. In this instance, though, I think the Celtic fans – those that were left – were whistling too, presumably for mercy. Anyway, as I noticed the referee, big Tom Wharton, studying his watch, I ran about a bit more than necessary just to be near the ball at the end. But, as it turned out, Billy McNeill was with it at the final whistle.

Billy picked up the ball, threw it over to me, and said: 'You'll be wanting this, Jim.' That was a pleasant gesture from Billy, even though that ball was the last thing *he* wanted.

I stuck it up my jumper, Baxter's imitation of a very pregnant woman, and walked off. Over came Tom 'Tiny' Wharton. He was always a very polite man, was Tom.

'May I have the ball, please, Mr Baxter?'

'Ball?' I said. 'What ball is that, Tom?' That was Baxter's imitation (very poor) of injured innocence. Well, Tom knew perfectly well I wasn't pregnant, didn't he? I had to tell him, in the end, that he wasn't getting it, and I marched into the dressing-room. There we toasted our success – and threw the ball around to each other.

Jimmy Millar then said: 'Let's give it to the auld yin.' He was referring to Ian McMillan, 32-year-old 'daddy' of Ibrox, the wee Prime Minister, who had just won his third cup-winners' medal and who was about to retire. So we gave him the ball. He had earned it. But soon afterwards the trouble began.

The secretary of the Scottish Football Association was Willie Allan, a pillar of the Church, a model of rectitude and, not to labour the point, I found him a pompous pain in the neck. I'm quite sure that he was an entirely efficient administrator, but to my mind he could just as easily have been the manager of a bank or building society. He had no real feeling for football. Indeed I heard a rumour at the time that he much preferred to go to Murrayfield than to Hampden, and I'm prepared to believe it.

We had just won another Cup Final, helping to bring in another small fortune to the SFA – and helping to pay his salary – and what did he do? He started crying about wanting the ball back. A few days later, when it had still not been returned to the SFA, he was quoted as saying:

'I don't care who has it – we want it back. The ball belongs to us, and if it doesn't turn up, we will take steps to see that it does. There is no question of the S.F.A. turning a blind eye to the incident. We will contact the clubs and ask them to trace it.'

You'd have thought it was a top detective talking to reporters about a vital murder clue. He went on, though, incredibly:

'If we were to ignore the business, then it would be a case of the law of the jungle taking over.'

Imagine that ... law of the jungle! But that was Oor Wullie. Everything by the rule-book. What would he ever have done without a rule-book? Maybe that's like asking what I would have done without my left foot. There's no answer, is there?

In the end, I gathered, they did get a ball back, but I very much doubt if it was the original match-ball. However, it would probably have been enough to keep Willie quiet. I hope Ian McMillan has the genuine article in a place of honour.

There's another cherished personal memory of that Cup Final replay – or rather of my preparation for it. It is not something which ought to be recommended to young players trying their best to make a profession of football. It would not be advised by the dedicated coaches and trainers of this world. We can all recognize that type, can we not? Their idea is that players should be sick through sheer physical effort, that, through pain, there is a sort of triumph.

Well, the way I spent the twenty-four hours prior to Rangers' demolition of Celtic in the Cup Final reply, would have turned all of those muscular, bawling coaches pale with horror. I will tell you why.

The previous night I had been to the pictures. At this stage, I ought to be able to recall the name of the film, you know, something really significant, like 'Gone with the Wind' or 'Mutiny on the *Bounty*' or 'The Cincinatti Kid'. In fact, the latter film hadn't been made in 1963, which is just as well. If I had seen it, with Steve McQueen locked in combat with Edward G. Robinson, I might never have made it to the game at all.

Well, I don't remember what the film was. I was far too concerned with wondering where the gambling game would be. I was still living with my folks in Fife, and I knew a fair bit about what went on in that part of the world, so, after the film, without waiting to salute 'God Save The Queen', I was off with some friends to what one could call a gambling shebeen. You could get a drink there, if you really wanted one. But it was the gambling that mattered. There was roulette, and there was 'chemmy'.

I played chemmy all night and took no drink. It was a well-respected company – most of it – comprising bookmakers and other assorted business men with a healthy cash-flow and a taste for the pasteboards. By breakfast-time on the day of the Cup Final replay, I had won a few bob more than £1,700.

It will be a long time before that kind of money can be regarded as something to scoff at. In 1963 it was a dream. Remember that I was earning, on the average, less than £2,000 a year basic with Rangers, and *that* still wasn't to be sneezed at, in Scottish terms.

I'm not very good at arithmetic, except when it comes to totting up a pay-packet and doubles and trebles, but in present-day terms, that £1,700 could not be worth a penny less than £15,000. There was also £600 in cheques owed to yours truly, but as any gambler knows, when you take a cheque instead of cash from somebody who is losing, that's the time to say goodbye to your money.

I got home to my folks in Fife at about half-past-nine in the morning, got a good breakfast, and went to bed for two hours. Was that unprofessional? Some might say it was. So far as I was concerned, the game that night was never going to be any bother. We had, remember, played Celtic the previous Saturday, and we knew what they could do, which wasn't very much.

I just might have been lucky in so far as the man immediately in front of me was wee Bobby Craig, the Celtic outside-right. The 'poison dwarf' we called him. He had short legs, and he was about as fast as me. And yet I don't really think it would have mattered if I had been directly opposed to a combination of Pele and Cruyff. I was right up there on top of the world, like James Cagney, only nobody blew me up. Every time I trapped the ball, every time I passed the ball to Jimmy or Ralph or Davie or wee Willie, I saw £1,700 in front of my eyes, and I could do no wrong.

I'm still not too pleased about some of the cheques.

4

The wonder of Wembley

Wembley is a very special place for all Scotsmen – or, at least, for all Scotsmen of my acquaintance. Moreover, those who disagree are not really Scottish. There is nothing quite like playing the English in their own backyard, and beating them. It is true that there are times when we don't beat them. That can happen, just like accidents can happen.

There was no accident in 1963. We had, of course, won the previous year. That was easy enough. It was Peter Wilson of the *Daily Mirror* who summed up the situation: 'Frankly, the game was so one-sided at times, the English fans should have got their money back.' (Interruption from J. Baxter: 'English fans? What English fans? Since when did we ever see English fans at Hampden, much less hear them?')

Mr Wilson, continuing:

> Poor Bobby Smith was the loneliest figure on that famous sward ... only big Billy McNeill to keep him company and take the ball away from him ... and behind him, two of the finest full backs ever to grace a Scottish jersey. If Alec Hamilton put a foot wrong at any time he must have tripped over the dressing-room step at half-time. Skipper Eric Caldow? Immense. Goalkeeper Bill Brown? Terrific – on the few occasions England were menacing.
>
> It was staggering to see the bemused expression grow on the faces of these much-lauded English stars, as they watched Jim Baxter execute a progressive 'Twist' marathon, smoothing down the divots with velvet feet before sliding into the area marked 'Danger'.

You will note the half-back line in the 1962 game, when Scotland beat England at Hampden for the first time in many a year. It was Crerand, McNeill, Baxter. The Press went quite potty about it. Yet the three of us hardly ever played again for Scotland as a line. Don't ask me why not.

All I'm saying is that the Scotland players of that particular era, 1962–63, were the best until that time, and since. We just might have won the World Cup, because we were better than the Czechs who, so luckily, beat us in a qualifying play-off – and lost only to Brazil in the final itself.

But let's move on to 1963, the first year I played at Wembley. The day before the game, I was looking over the park and saying to myself, and to a few reporters who happened to be about: 'If I can't play well on turf like that, I'll get a job selling brushes round the doors.'

I had heard all sorts of stories about players being injured because of the very lushness of the turf. It seemed to me then, and still does, that they must have been careless or unable to turn correctly. The grass is certainly a little longer and thicker than is normal on most football pitches, but not so much so that the ball can't be controlled. Put it this way: it didn't bother Scotland that afternoon.

It didn't bother me, that's for sure. Two-goal Baxter! I'm a gambler, but I wouldn't have accepted 20–1 against my scoring a couple of goals in my first game against England at Wembley. What about 33–1? Well, possibly. But not confidently.

Here's a good pub-question, by the way. Who was the first player to score against Gordon Banks in an international match? Who was the *second* player to score against Gordon Banks in an international match? Answer to both questions: J.B.

Yes, that was the international debut of Gordon Banks, destined to be recognized as the greatest goalkeeper in the world bar none. And imagine Baxter scoring two goals. Sorry to go on about that, but you can't blame

Here's JB at three years old, with my Mum and
Dad, Agnes and Robert

No prizes at all for identifying JB . . . the team is Crossgates Primrose

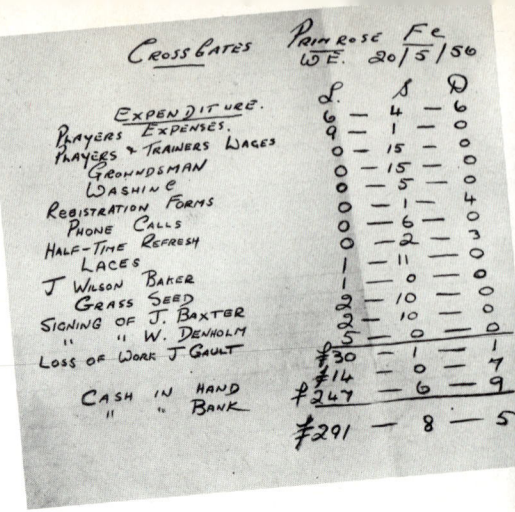

Above: Signing of James Baxter by Crossgates Primrose for £2 10s. Well, they got their money back

Left: I'm in the army now – that's me on the left, in case you were wondering

Below: Signing of James Baxter by Sunderland – watched by Scot Symon (*left*) and Ian McColl

The Rangers, 1960. Baxter is a new boy, third from left. I wish I could remember why they're all applauding

How about this, then? Baxter is actually tackling! And it looks as if I got the ball

The shame of Seville! I wonder why I bothered to read about it. I had the bruises to prove it all

Mackay, Ure and Baxter – all in Scotland jerseys. Well, it wasn't the worst half-back line, was it?

Goodbye, Vienna! Broken leg and all – but at least one happy memory!

me, surely. After all, I had never before scored twice in a top-class competitive game, and I had never before taken a penalty in a senior game.

Remember, too, that England had a very fair side at that time. Banks needs no more praise from me. Jimmy Armfield always looked as if he were smoking a pipe, with his carpet slippers on, but he was a fine full-back. Gerry Byrne was, admittedly, overrated: Willie Henderson took poor Gerry to the cleaners so often that he should have asked for a receipt. But then there was Bobby Moore – and it doesn't matter how much stick Bobby Moore took from the Scottish fans, he was some footballer, fit to take an honourable place in any company. Big Maurice Norman of Tottenham was unfairly underrated by too many people, but Ron Flowers of Wolves, although ordinary against us that day, was an excellent wing-half. In attack England had such players as Jimmy Greaves, Bobby Smith and Bobby Charlton, and I bet they'd be glad of any one of that lot today.

In all my life, I never saw a player so good in the penalty-box as Jimmy Greaves. He was so cool that you suspected he was too thick to think. Such suspicion was soon seen off as soon as you met the man, but he remained difficult to understand. It was as if he had been born to score goals, a kind of machine. He didn't panic, even under the worst stress. He almost never made mistakes. When you saw him moving into the box, it was a joy – just so long as he wasn't moving into *your* penalty-box.

These days he had been building a new career for himself as a TV commentator in company with Ian St. John – who also played, and played well, in 1963. I really do hope that Jimmy makes a big success of TV, a permanent success. He was a genius . . . an overworked word usually, but in his case hardly adequate.

Bobby Charlton opposed us too, and there's nothing I can say about Charlton that hasn't been said countless times before. An admirable man as well as a very great player.

Bobby Smith? Well, I respected Bobby, but that was the afternoon he was carried off, along with Eric Caldow. Bobby came back on to the field. Eric didn't. You don't play on with a broken leg. I'm sorry to say that I blamed Bobby Smith for Caldow's injury, and I'm not alone in that.

Somebody wrote about that match: 'Just as we got the news that Caldow was in hospital with a broken leg, Jim Baxter took the game over. He must have heard the news.' In fact, I didn't know at that moment, although I did fear the worst.

I put the first nail in England's coffin at the half-hour mark. After Willie Henderson scampered past Flowers, Byrne went in to challenge him and was left looking as if he had just missed the last bus on a rainy night. Then Willie belted the ball across goal, where Jimmy Armfield was waiting.

Now when I took on Armfield, I didn't think I'd win. But Jimmy's concentration lapsed. He must have been looking for a match for his pipe. I was never as bad a tackler as a lot of folk believed, but I still had no right to take the ball from such an experienced player. However, that's exactly what I did, and when Banks came out, I stroked the ball in between him and the post. It was quite a simple goal, but a goal I will not forget if I live to be ninety, which I almost certainly won't.

A couple of minutes later, Willie Henderson was on his way again, and when I saw Ron Flowers challenge, I could visualize in advance what was going to happen. Ron was not known for a good-natured attitude towards clever wingers and, right on cue, he hammered Henderson into the Wembley turf. A penalty all the way.

I should explain at this point that, although Eric Caldow was officially team captain, the real captain was Dave Mackay. Even if Eric had still been on the field, I fancy Dave would have said to me what he did say:

'There's the ball, Jim. You know what to do with it.' I knew what to do with it all right. No problem. No nerves – at least, not that I can remember.

THE WONDER OF WEMBLEY

Many sports writers were saying after our win that we had the talent to return to Wembley, for the World Cup Final in 1966, but that wasn't to be. All the same, the players of that time are worth recalling, because, I repeat, since the 1962–63 period we have not had their equal.

Consider these names: Bill Brown, Eric Caldow, Alec Hamilton, Dave Mackay, Paddy Crerand, Ian Ure, Billy McNeill, Willie Henderson, John White, Ian St. John, Alex Scott, Denis Law, Davie Wilson. What would a Scottish team manager give today for just a handful of talent in that class?

More specifically: was it not a scandal that somebody like Dave Mackay received only a few Scotland caps? Dave was a veritable giant among the players of the 1960s, a born leader. John White, rather like Kenny Dalglish in the 1980s, was seldom accorded by Scottish fans the respect he deserved. Yet he was a true artist. Every other professional admired him. If he was on the ball, and you ran into a space, you just *knew* he would bounce that ball at your feet.

Denis Law was, and is, legendary. If anybody ever makes a list of the half-dozen best forwards of all time, and leaves out Denis, he should be jailed for ten years with nothing to read but a copy of Sir Alf Ramsey's memoirs. And Ian St. John, a member of the mighty Liverpool side created by the incomparable Bill Shankly, didn't need to be six feet tall – although he was a high-class centre-forward, by any standards. Nobody proved more conclusively the theory that brain can always beat brawn.

Well, perhaps that last statement could be challenged – on behalf of the Scotland side which beat England 3–2 on 15 April 1967. To this day, many Scots call that 'Baxter's international', and obviously this makes me very proud indeed. For while I insist that the players of four years previously were better, the actual occasion in 1967 was very, very special.

Think of it. Only nine months before, England had

won the World Cup. I know that there are several sound reasons for doubting the genuine merit of England's success, but that's not the point. The point is that their name was on the cup, and they believed they were the best football team on earth. We knew better, and we were determined to let the rest of the world know, too. To us, and to most right-thinking Scots, England's status didn't make any sense. After all, it hadn't been so long since we'd grown tired of beating them.

That was a strange-looking team, all the same. I wonder how many of the fans who went wild about us could now reel off the names. Ronnie Simpson of Celtic, who must have been on the verge of drawing the pension, yet still an exceptional goalkeeper, was soon to win a European Cup-winners' medal. So was big Tam Gemmell, a great character who had about as much respect for authority as yours truly had. Eddie McCreadie of Chelsea was the other full-back – they were still called full-backs then – and it was a Rangers half-back line: John Greig, Ronnie McKinnon and myself. Anyway, I always remember it as a Rangers trio, even though I was playing for Sunderland at the time. The forwards were Willie Wallace (Celtic), Billy Bremner (Leeds) – maybe I'm stretching it a bit to call Billy a forward – Jim McCalliog (Sheffield Wednesday), Denis Law (Manchester United) and Bobby Lennox (Celtic).

Now if you consider that team in advance, and then cast an eye over the great names of England, it just had to be a canter for England. That's what they thought, too. But as I said, the score was 3–2, and it could quite easily have been 13–2. So why didn't we rub it in? Why didn't we bury the English under an avalanche of goals? We could have done, oh yes. No bother. But the choice was ours. By that, I mean the choice was down to Bremner, Law and myself.

Naturally, I've had lots of arguments since, with people who didn't like the way we took the mickey. I don't think they understood, I really don't. A team and a country can forget big scores against them. Such things can happen, if one side has an off-day and the other a good day . . . or if there's an unusual element of luck. Our aim was to show England how *easily* we could beat them. We wanted to give them no excuses. We wanted the Scottish punters to laugh at the English as well as to enthuse over victory. Which is exactly what happened.

Deliberately, we kept the game on a razor's edge, staying that wee bit ahead on goals, stroking the ball about, everying designed to indicate that, if we felt like it, we would score a few more.

We know that England did put forward some kind of excuse in that Jackie Charlton was off for a little while in the first half, and resumed at centre-forward. It was a pathetic, transparent excuse and still is. I'll tell you this, big Jackie wasn't bad for somebody who was supposed to have a suspected broken toe. Ronnie Simpson had only two real saves in that first half, and one of them was from Charlton. Then he actually did score late in the game. Some passenger! In fact, England's excuse seems thinner than ever, if it is borne in mind that Charlton was probably one of just two or three Englishmen we had to watch.

Why were England so bad? That's the wrong question. It should be: why were Scotland so good? I'll answer that. We had better football players, which isn't exactly a small advantage. And we weren't afraid.

England had played nineteen games without defeat. They were well-organized and they were quite physical. We were organized, too, but never rigidly. And if it came to handing out stick, well, that was all right, too. Not that it was a dirty match – despite wee Alan Ball. He kept on confusing my shins with the ball. He was running about, demented, like a fart in a bottle.

Billy Bremner had told us before the match that Alan was nicknamed Jimmy Clitheroe, because of his high, squeaky voice. Billy had also told us that it was a nickname greatly resented. So, naturally, that's what we shouted to him, throughout the match. He wasn't the only Englishman to go daft that day – Jackie Charlton wasn't in the best of moods either, and Nobby Stiles, minus those front teeth, looked as if he could cheerfully have killed us all. But only Ball kept on kicking. Maybe Bremner shouldn't have asked him: 'D'you think you'll be a player, when your voice breaks?'

In the second half, when we had established beyond reasonable doubt that we could win looking round, I indulged in 'keepy-uppy', thereby enraging the English even more. Now and again one of us would put a foot on the ball, then walk away from it as if we were bored with the whole affair. Of course, we knew that a team-mate would get there first.

You can imagine how the fans loved it all. The Scottish fans, I mean. And in a way, that might have been the best aspect of all. To win at Wembley means even more than to win at Hampden, and I'm as Scottish as anybody. It's the match most eagerly anticipated by the Scottish supporters, most of whom save up for two years to go south and then blow the lot. To lose in front of such wonderful fans is to let them down.

After that 1967 match, I remember Sir Alf Ramsey saying: 'I warned it would take a great team to beat us. Let's give them their due.' That was nice of him.

Bobby Brown, our own manager, said that everything had gone to plan. He was right, of course, but I hope enough time has passed for Bobby to accept that he didn't have much to do with it. I'm not being unkind, just truthful. We all liked Bobby. He was the perfect gentleman, which was perhaps half of his problem as a team manager. He didn't have a strong personality like, say, Jock Wallace or Tommy Docherty or Jock Stein. If he suggested a particular tactic before a match, and if Denis or Billy or I disagreed, he would immediately change it. I couldn't imagine 'The Doc' even listening to disagreement, and his record later as Scotland's manager still stands well.

Hundreds, maybe thousands, of fans ran on to the pitch afterwards, and that reminds me of a story which I don't think has been told before. The players were supposed to go to the Café Royal for the official banquet, a duty appearance and hardly an occasion of unconfined celebration. So Denis Law and I arranged to meet Dave Mackay in one of the bars at the Café Royal, just as soon as we could decently slip away from the banquet. This we duly did, and when we arrived at the appointed bar, we couldn't believe our eyes. Dave was there, with about a dozen of his pals from Edinburgh. They were all sitting round a table, getting stuck into the 'bevy'. But was astonished us was the 'tablecloth'. It consisted entirely of pieces of Wembley turf, that unmistakeable, lush, green Wembley turf. It goes without saying that Denis and I joined in with a will.

5

Good-night, Vienna

Most people, when hearing the name Vienna, probably think of the Danube, Strauss waltzes and those immense chocolate-cream pastries for which the city is famous. Me, I remember a broken leg. It was in a European Cup-tie, Rangers against Vienna Rapid, and we were a goal up from the first leg at Ibrox. I remember just about every detail of that trip.

We flew into Vienna on the Sunday and, as the plane landed, we couldn't see anything except thick, swirling snow. The date was 6 December 1964. The game was due to be played two days later. Very few of us thought there was an even chance of it taking place. And the Viennese, following the Continental pattern, were walking around with long faces, partly because of the weather – so they said – partly because they were worried about their team. Again, so they said.

Rapid had just managed to beat the unrated Wiener Newstadt 1–0 on the Saturday, and their captain, Halla, was supposed to be unfit. Our own Saturday game, against Morton, had been postponed by fog, and when the Viennese heard this, they adopted cynical attitudes. Perhaps they thought Scot Symon had arranged the fog, and that, despite my admiration for our manager, was unquestionably beyond even his capabilities. All this Viennese cynicism and supposed pessimism had not prevented the sale of 50,000 tickets. We had no doubt that, below the surface, Rapid were confidently expecting to win.

On the Monday the more lyrical of the scribes in the official party were describing Vienna as a winter wonderland, millions of lights reflected upon a thick carpet of snow . . . that kind of thing. We didn't see much wonderful about the situation. It seemed that the Viennese were utterly determined that the game would go on, come hell, high water or blizzard. And there *was* a blizzard that day. We trained in it, on a small ground near the famous Prater Stadium, scene of the big match – and itself inches deep in snow.

There was much arguing, apparently, among the Viennese officials, about when they should try to clear the pitch, or *if* they should clear it. They had hundreds of soldiers standing by, complete with shovels. In the end it was decided to wait until the following day and to do whatever was necessary, which would depend on what nature did overnight. The only sure thing was that we would be playing on a surface guaranteed to be very dodgy, by any standards. The Tuesday was a holiday, the number of tickets sold had increased to 70,000, and it had to be doubtful whether the Viennese would call the game off for anything less than a fair-sized earthquake.

In the end there was some rain, and the pitch was as soft as one of those Viennese pastries. Being captain, I took a sizeable responsibility for tactics, although I would probably have done so anyway, captain or not. I knew that Rapid were experts at the offside trap, and I knew they would be trying it on as often as they could. Above all, I knew that we would have to keep the pace slow. There could be no point in running about at 90 m.p.h. on that kind of pitch.

At first, it wasn't easy. Every Rangers player was on the top of his form, but that offside trap! I didn't count at the time, having better things to do, but somebody did work out later on that we were caught out no fewer than 26 times. Not all, by any means, were genuine offside decisions, but the Hungarian referee said they were, and nothing else counted.

I'm not going to pick out the best Rangers players that

afternoon, apart from mentioning that it was Willie Johnston's first big game abroad. It took us nearly 20 minutes to beat the trap, and I had something to do with it. I managed to beat three of the Austrians – how's that for modesty? – and noted that Jim Forrest was onside. I couldn't be sure that the referee would see it the same way, but I took the chance and gave Jim the ball. He scored a superb goal.

It was now obvious – painfully so to Rapid – that anybody with possession of the ball had a big advantage. The idea was to let go of the ball only at the right time, and to take the ball past an opponent. Tankers could have turned quicker than the Viennese defenders in the mush and slush, and they simply didn't have players good enough to exploit the conditions. We did, and we ended up taking the mickey out of them, especially after Davie Wilson had made the score 2–0. I don't think Rangers have ever played so well in Europe, and if you want to include Barcelona in that assessment, that's all right with me. To get a draw against a good team away from home in Europe is always interpreted as a marvellous result. To win 2–0 in the Prater Stadium was fantastic.

Why do I stress the value of a good performance away from home? A good question, and one to which I have no real answer except to say that it has long been accepted that a team plays better, with greater confidence, at home – especially so in Europe. It is not, however, accepted by me.

I have never been a manager, but, had I been, I would have tried to change the tradition. As far as I am concerned, a football park is a football park, wherever it may be. If you can play at all, what does it matter whether you're in Glasgow or Moscow. I have never worried about the other side, anyway. My idea has always been to let them worry about us. If you lack confidence, you're liable to be beaten by people with less talent who *do* believe in themselves. But too many players away from home, and not only in foreign parts, are looking for excuses in advance. They say they can't sleep in a strange bed, they say the travelling upsets their routine, they say they can't eat the food. This is a load of rubbish, and it's time managers – who are responsible for much of the brainwashing – recognized this. The problem is, managers are also seeking excuses.

To be very fair, Scot Symon was a most honourable exception to that rule. In Vienna, as in League matches back home, Scot was simple in his instructions – leaving anything else to me. It was only common sense to contain Rapid for the first half-hour or so, while continually watching for chances to have a go. When Jim Forrest put that first one away, I knew, I *knew*, that the match and the tie was ours. At the end the Viennese were cheering Rangers and jeering their own players. Some were throwing snowballs in their disgust. But when that final whistle went, James Baxter had other things to think about.

There were about 30 seconds, no more, to go. I was strolling towards the tunnel, keeping a sort of fatherly eye on the proceedings, wondering who we would be playing in the semi-final, when the ball came over towards me. Throughout the whole game I had been enjoying lots of space, and enjoying every minute of the match too. This was the exception. I don't know where Walter Skocik came from. All I knew was what I heard. The crack! There's something quite memorable about hearing your own leg break. For a couple of seconds, I stayed upright, then down I went. It was very sore.

Even in the pain, I felt really fed up, realizing that I wouldn't be playing any more football for some time yet. Davie Kinnear and Joe Craven came racing over. 'For God's sake, Davie, leave it,' I said. 'It's broken. Just leave it.' Was it a fair tackle? I don't think so. But I don't believe, either, that Skocik intended to break my leg. There have been a few footballers in my experience who would break a fellow-player's leg deliberately, but they are very few and far between. They are despised. And Walter Skocik wasn't one of them.

Also, I had given him a terrible time. I must have 'nutmegged' him a couple of dozen times. He had been chasing me like a man demented all afternoon, just like wee Alan Ball at Wembley and with no more success. When I look back, I can say to myself that if he had done to me what I did to him, I'd have broken his neck, never mind his leg! The following morning he came up to the hospital, with his girlfriend and some flowers. He was almost crying, and I felt really sorry for him.

Meanwhile, the local Press and TV were going daft. All they could talk about, it seemed, was 'Jeem Baxter, Jeem Baxter'. Well, it was nice to be appreciated, and it made me feel a lot better. Oh yes, I was the hero of the game Anybody who is captain of a side that wins away from home in Europe and breaks a leg in the last minute is bound to be a hero. But of all the games I ever played for Rangers, that one just might be my best. A lot of other folk thought so too, not excepting the Austrian coach, Bimbo Binder, who said I was top-bracket world-class. One Viennese TV commentator said they hadn't seen anything like it since Pele, which isn't faint praise.

It was also on the following day that I had to remonstrate with the Austrian doctor, the one who had put the plaster cast on my right leg. He had to cut the plaster, to allow for muscle movement, before completing the operation with a plastic bandage. As he began to cut around the fibula, the small bone above the ankle, where the break was, the pain really grabbed me. I have to confess that I told him what I thought of him, and in the kind of language you might hear in a Fife pit on being thumped on the elbow by a careless colleague's hammer. Scot Symon was in the room.

'Jim, Jim,' said Scot, 'the doctor understands English.' Maybe he did, but did he understand Scottish, Fifestyle? I didn't care much.

'It's all right for him, boss,' I said, 'but it's my leg.' Of course, I was being unfair to the doctor who was doing his best. Suddenly I realized the comic side of the situation, and burst out laughing. So did the doc!

GOOD-NIGHT, VIENNA

I should have flown home with the official party from Vienna, but the airport was out of action because of fog. It was decided that we should drive the 200 miles to Salzburg, which was in operation. The official story of what happened then, is as follows.

Another doctor said I was fit enough to make the seven-hour journey by ambulance. Accompanied in the ambulance by Eric Caldow, who had a badly bruised leg, and Norrie Martin, I was bounced about on the cobbles. About 40 miles out of Vienna, I decided I had had enough. The pain was getting worse by the minute, and I was anxious in case the bumping and bouncing might aggravate the injury. It didn't help when the driver said he was going to fasten snow-chains to the wheels of the ambulance.

'You can do what you like', I told him, 'and you can go where you like. I'm not going any further, and that's final.' He didn't like this. Probably he was on overtime rates. But a message was sent to the Rangers bus, which was in front of us.

Scot Symon agreed that I could go back to Vienna, very slowly, in the ambulance. After all, I was valuable to Rangers, and they didn't want me out of the game for any longer than was absolutely necessary. So I went to Salzburg later, by train. As I said, that's the official, published story. Later on in this book, I will tell the real story about why I stopped the ambulance.

6

Transfer truths

I think it was Don Revie who said, when he was the manager of Leeds: 'I'd just love to have Jim Baxter in my team. There's just one problem – I love my sleep even more. When I go to bed, I want to sleep. I don't want to lie awake, waiting for the phone to ring and for somebody to tell me that Jim has been thrown out of somewhere or punched somebody or been punched.'

Frankly, I wouldn't blame Don if these were, in fact, the exact words he used. I was a good mate of his. We used to play a lot of golf together every summer – that was in the days when a footballer was allowed a decent holiday. But maybe he just knew me too well.

After I'd been with Rangers about three years, I started a kind of campaign. It was aimed at getting more money – or a transfer to England. At that time, 1963, I was earning £35 basic a week, plus the permitted League bonuses. It all worked out, with the half-yearly performance bonuses, to a little less than £3,000 a year. Now when you remember that Rangers were pulling in 50,000 for a League game to Ibrox, and as many as 80,000 for a really big game, that was a ridiculous wage. In current terms, I'd estimate it as the equivalent of about £200 a week.

Of course, I was a long way from the breadline. I would not want to be misunderstood. I was well off, single, and enjoying myself. I could have got anything I wanted in Glasgow, and I did. With one exception . . .

Rangers refused to pay me the money I believed I was worth. I was not lacking in respect for my colleagues, then or now, but there is no doubt that I was the biggest attraction in Scottish football. There's no such thing as a one-man team, and there never will be. But can it be seriously denied that certain players pull in higher gates than others?

One newspaper polled its readers, asking the question: 'Do you think Baxter is worth £100 a week, or should he go to England?' That was the 1963 figure I had decided on. Well, the replies were unanimous. Every letter said I was worth the money. Let me quote from one of them: 'As a Celtic fan, the sooner Jim Baxter leaves Rangers, the better. It would give us a fighting chance of beating them. Baxter is a wonderful player, a crowd-puller and a personality. He is entitled to a higher wage than any of his team-mates.'

Note that last point. But I stress again that I wasn't really interested in what my team-mates were getting. It was none of my business. My pay-packet was very *much* my business. Directors like Baillie Wilson and John Lawrence, however, would say: 'Oh no, we're all Rangers together.' That was true – though it didn't sound too convincing coming from people who were never likely to be hard up as long as they lived. Meanwhile, Billy Stevenson – the man I displaced in the Rangers team – was down at Liverpool picking up at least twice as much as I was. That was none of my business, either, but it was common knowledge, and it really got to me.

Johnny Haynes was on £100 at Fulham, and, while I had a lot of time for Haynes, nobody put him in my class as a crowd-puller. After all, Fulham were playing in front of about 15,000 people, then.

In England, of course, players negotiated their own wages, or at least they did at Tottenham. You learn things, travelling around with the Anglos in the Scottish squad! That's the way it should have been in Scotland and at Ibrox. Suppose, for instance, Billy Ritchie, our goalkeeper, had gone upstairs to Scot Symon and negotiated more money than my own wage – and supposing he had come back down the stairs and told me so. Do you think I'd have flown into a temper? Believe me, I'd have said: 'Good luck to you, Billy.'

There was another thing that preyed on my mind. Willie McNaught, whom I had idolized at Raith Rovers, had spent 20 years in the game, and if he had played for Rangers, he'd have won dozens of caps. And what did he have to show for these 20 years? When I put in my first transfer request, he was back at his old trade as a bricklayer!

Also, these were my best years. I was turning it on every week, and we were winning just about every week. Rangers were making a fortune, paying 20% dividends (and often a 10% bonus). Yet they still treated us as comparative peasants. The directors and some officials talked about Rangers being an institution, with hard-and-fast rules and traditions. Why, they bleated, should they change their rules for one man?

My answer was that they were out of date. Alan Morton and Davie Meiklejohn weren't playing any more. Rangers were mixing with the great clubs of the world. And it was high time they conceded that the twentieth century had actually arrived. So I moaned and moaned. To no avail. That year I was even picked for the Rest of the World squad to play in England's centenary match. The only other Scot was Denis Law. But I still got only £35 a week from Rangers. When I re-signed for the 1963–64 season, it was on the understanding that, if any club came for me, then the offer would be seriously considered.

Stoke City, I learned, were anxious to sign me for £70,000, but Rangers said it wasn't enough. Which is almost funny when you think of it. If I was worth so much money, why didn't they recognize it when they paid me my wages?

But the real sickener was when Tottenham Hotspur made an approach – and the deal fell through. It was all arranged by Jim Rodger, a sports writer who fully deserved the nickname of 'Scoop'. Bill Nicholson, the Spurs manager, met me at the Boulevard Hotel in Glasgow.

We agreed on the terms. Later, Bill met Scot Symon and, presumably, some Ibrox directors. I was elated. My job was to replace Danny Blanchflower at White Hart Lane. No small feat, but well within my capability.

Then something happened. To this day, I don't know what went wrong, but I strongly suspect that, in the end, stories about my life-style changed Nicholson's mind. And I don't suppose the Rangers representatives tried too hard to influence him otherwise.

Of course, I was depressed. But I'd have been suicidal if I had thought for a minute that my ability on the park had had anything to do with the breakdown of the transfer. Well, I didn't think that – not for a second, never mind a minute. All I could do was to keep doing my best for Rangers, and hope that something would turn up.

Sunderland turned up. I had just put in my third successive transfer request. It was the summer of 1965, and I was to be married in June. I was becoming desperate for a move, although Rangers had, by this time, increased my money to a princely £45 a week. It was all about money. It was never a question of *wanting* to leave Rangers or Scotland. It was a question of being forced to go for solid financial reasons.

The transfer to Sunderland took place in the North British Hotel in Edinburgh. Looking back with the benefit of hindsight, I could hardly have made a worse move.

That summer, I well remember telling reporters 'Sunderland will suit me down to the ground. This is one of the most famous clubs in English football, with a tremendous tradition. They are fighting to build a side equal to the great Roker teams of the past. It is now my ambition to help them do just that.' Nor was I alone in believing that this would be a wonderful new challenge which I was well equipped to meet and surmount. Just about every sports writer in Scotland – and plenty in England too – shared my opinion.

For example, the *Sun*:

> Wearsiders have a hero who will add a new dimension to their enjoyment of football. He's different!
>
> On the field, no matter the company, Jim Baxter is different. Even in the way he dresses, with the briefest of shorts, hitched up to make them briefer still . . . he's as brash and modern as tomorrow. His dress is as mod as his play, though . . . flashy and up-to-date.

Other writers examined Ibrox and wondered if the gap would be filled. Or if it *could* be filled. The *Daily Express* headline was: 'Ibrox Worry: Who Replaces Baxter?' The text: 'Bewildered Ibrox fans are asking that question . . . but Rangers and their fans must face up to the fact that they cannot quickly just unearth "another Baxter".' Yet another paper said, simply: 'The king is gone . . . long live the king!'

Now of course, that was all very well and heart-warming indeed. Not, however, flattering. Every comment was well justified, as I knew very well. I'm still leaving modesty to those with a lot to be modest about. Anyway, think of what Sir Matt Busby was also saying at that time: 'Jim is world class. His greatest asset is that no matter the state of the game, *his* team begins to play all over again once he has the ball.' And Billy McNeill, then captain of Celtic and Scotland: 'Jim is the most creative footballer in the country.' I didn't really have to blow that trumpet by myself, did I?

There was a warning note from Denis Law: 'Once Jim settles into English football, he'll really enjoy it. But he'll find it a lot different.' But if these words from Denis *were* intended as a warning, there wasn't much I could do about it. The die was cast, and the £80,000 cheque was signed.

That apart, I wasn't in the mood for listening to warnings from anybody. Certainly my financial situation improved dramatically. Of that £80,000 transfer fee, I received about £11,000. Don't forget we're talking about nearly 20 years ago. It was very nice money then, and wouldn't be too bad now, when I think of it. Also, my wage was a basic £80, an immediate jump of £35. Then, perhaps above all, there were the bonuses. These were £40 a point, plus appearance money for the F.A. Cup, appearance money even for the League Cup, and a special bonus for a reasonable place in the League table.

If I'd been playing in a good team at Sunderland, I'd have been a rich man. But believe me, I was *not* playing in a good team. That was the trouble. As I said before, there's no such thing as a one-man side, but not long after I arrived at Roker Park, it was evident that that was the role expected of me.

7

Second-rate Roker

I don't suppose this is going to sound kind, but I'm afraid that my move to Sunderland from Rangers was a bit like going to the Partick Thistle of England. I hope my many friends round Maryhill way will forgive me for that, but you have to be realistic.

No doubt the Sunderland board was ambitious enough. If the directors had been a stick-in-the-mud bunch, they wouldn't have paid £80,000 – a mammoth sum then – for Jim Baxter. But the side of 1965 was still ordinary, because the players were ordinary. They had Charlie Hurley, a king on Wearside at the time. Well, Charlie was a sound, competent player who would never move out of the middle. Others, such as Cecil Irvine, Len Ashurst and Jimmy McNab, were no more than honest pros. When I saw who was going to be playing centre-forward, I had to laugh. Nicky Sharkey was a nice lad, and not untalented, but he was just 5 ft 6 in tall. In the English First Division, mind you! It was incredible. Giving a good pass to a six-footer who is being marked English-style is hard enough, even now, but what chance of getting wee Nicky going?

Mike Hellawell was there, too, an English internationalist. I liked Mike. He enjoyed a bet on the horses, so we had an obvious fellow-feeling. But it was about all Mike did think about, and although he could run like a deer on the field, he wasn't too hard to discourage. Lots of speed-merchants are like that, and I can't blame them. If they are slowed down, they don't have much left, and they know it.

Sunderland had just previously won promotion from the Second Division, and Ian McColl had taken over as manager. I've got a lot of respect for Ian as a man, and so does everybody else who really knows him, but he was never strong enough as a football manager. In a way he was like Bobby Brown: he was easily swayed. Yet you really have to be something of a tyrant when you're dealing with people like me. Or, if not a tyrant, at least someone like Scot Symon who could be diplomatic, but who had a backbone of steel. Although I've related elsewhere the liberties I took at Ibrox, there was still a line you didn't cross.

You see, one of the very first things a manager has to create is pride, personal and professional pride. Jock Wallace and Jock Stein call it character, others call it self-confidence, but in the end it's pride. It's imperative, when you walk out onto that park, to feel on top of the job, to feel you're going to win, whatever the opposition. Once you let the other lot intimidate you, you've lost.

Why have Rangers and Celtic won so much in Scottish football over the years? Of course, they have often had better players, but not always. No, their greatest asset has been a feeling of in-built superiority. In recent times Dundee United and Aberdeen have come to be called the 'New Firm', but they'll need another half-century or so before they can achieve the mental state usually taken for granted at Ibrox and Parkhead.

Naturally, all this rubs off on the opposition and does them no good at all. I wonder how many goals' start the royal blue or the green-and-white hoops have been worth in the last century. Some folk talk of how the Old Firm – by its very existence – influences referees. Maybe there's some truth in that. But that kind of influence is rarely necessary. Other teams are intimidated before they leave the dressing-room – by reputations and, no doubt, through brain-washing by the Press.

This looked obvious enough when I was playing for Rangers, but it was never more embarrassingly emphasized than on the day Tottenham Hotspur came up to play at Roker Park. The Spurs players trooped off the bus, chatting happily to each other, lords of creation dressed in the very best, with haircuts that probably cost as much as the shoes the Sunderland players were wearing.

That's when I noticed the looks on the faces of my team-mates, as they watched Dave Mackay, Jimmy Greaves and the rest saunter to the players' entrance. I couldn't believe it. Dave was greeting me like a long-lost brother, arranging refreshment for later that evening, and the Sunderland guys had their mouths hanging open. It was as if they were wee boys who had unexpectedly been allowed to tap a ball around with the men. I do not jest . . . I could visualize them asking the Spurs team for autographs.

Imagine an attitude like that towards a team which we were about to meet on equal terms. It was an attitude I heartily detested. Sometimes, on the park, I'd shout, 'Come on, let's take the mickey out of this lot!' It was pure frustration on my part, and I was probably hoping to set an example, to instil *some* pride into them. Some hope!

It was a simple matter of ability and, with very few exceptions, they just didn't have it. They were born hero-worshippers, and not only of Tottenham. Any big name. Arsenal, Manchester United, even Everton. How we stayed in the First Division that season, I'll never know. We were continually struggling, and it was just as well that we carried a lot of luck.

It is no exaggeration to say that there were times when I felt I was back at Raith Rovers. Still wearing the No. 6, it was my responsibility – as it had been with Rangers – to give the forwards plenty of the ball. But whereas with Rangers a pass upfield would, more often than not, stay up there for a while and maybe produce a goal, the ball tended to come straight back again at Sunderland. As I say, just like Raith days. So I had to beware of following up on a pass, of looking for the return; because it was odds on that the ball would come whizzing past me, and

I'd be chasing.

Yet despite all that, I didn't find it harder to play in the English First Division than in Scotland. I wasn't exactly enamoured with the amount of chasing backwards I had to do, but I retained the gift for making space for myself. Also, the calibre of players did improve eventually.

When I arrived at Roker, there was a clique led by Charlie Hurley with whom, as you may have suspected, I was never the best of friends. Besides Charlie, there was Bobby McNab and Martin Harvey. They were the guv'-nors, you might say. Well, that wasn't a situation likely to be appreciated by J.B., and I like to think I put it right. Or, from Charlie's point of view, wrong.

The very fact that Ian McColl, who had signed me, was manager, did help. I teamed up with George Mulhall who really *could* play and, later, Neil Martin came down from Hibs. When Sunderland signed my cousin, George Kinnell, that was the icing on my cake. Now there was a new set of guv'nors and, not long afterwards, Sunderland had the good sense to sign Colin Todd, a great player. Even my old Ibrox team-mate, Ralphie Brand, arrived, and, at long last, we were beginning to look like a team.

It was a pity about the cliques, all the same. They should never be necessary among professionals. If I did help to form the second and dominant one, it was partly accidental, partly a matter of self-defence. Cliques are bad for dressing-room atmosphere. There was no open hostility at Roker, just this niggling, no-talking nonsense. I couldn't stand that. It was always my habit to speak frankly. I might say to somebody: 'You're not worth your place, you're a waster.'

But I would say such things usually in another fit of frustration, after I'd spent 90 minutes doing my absolute best – and watching others definitely not doing their best, hiding. And I never bore grudges. After everything had been brought out into the open, and a few harsh words exchanged, that would be it. It would work both ways. I wouldn't bear a grudge if one of my team-mates turned on me and gave me a mouthful. I would snap back – especially if his criticism had been justified – but I'd be happy to shake hands.

I have to say, in no spirit of gloating, that we had one of our better spells when Charlie Hurley was dropped, and when the second 'clique' was more or less in control. The team that earned quite a bit of praise in my second season at Roker would usually read something like this: Montgomery: Parke, Ashurst: Todd, Kinnell, Baxter: Herd, Suggett, Martin, Heslop and Brand or Mulhall.

In my second season at Sunderland there was, of course, the Scottish 3–2 victory over the 'world champions', England, and I couldn't have been playing too badly. That is confirmed not only by the fact that I was picked at all for the England game, but by the great expectations heaped on me *before* that game. I'll not easily forget what wee Jack Adams wrote on the morning of Wembley, in the *Daily Record*:

'Jim Baxter will be the giant of Wembley this afternoon . . . the annual battle against England has become a personal crusade for Baxter. He has arrogance, artistry, a skill that can only be inborn . . . now he also has a cause . . . to prove that ten men and true plus Jim Baxter more than equal the world champions.'

Well, Mr Adams proved a fair prophet, but there was reasonable evidence for the prophecy. Sunderland had had a run of 12 matches without defeat, and you needn't take my word for it that I had something to do with it. Charlie Summerbell, one of the top scribes in the north-east, was not among my intimate circle of mates. Nevertheless he wrote: 'We got off on the wrong foot at the start . . . and since then we have regarded each other with mutual disrespect . . . but honesty demands of me that Baxter should be given credit for the part he has played in Sunderland's successful run . . . he is the shop steward of the Roker revival . . . the mainspring . . . a tantalizing expert on the field and an unapproachable – and, it seems, insensitive – character off the pitch.'

SECOND-RATE ROKER

A sting in the tail, there, right enough. But then our Charlie wrote: 'He [Baxter] would be unwise to ignore the adulation that is his for the asking and the sublime satisfaction that comes from being absorbed in a small-knit community.'

Well, nearly a couple of decades have passed since that appeared in print. The first part of it was true, but I'm still a little hurt by the second part. It implies that I looked on the folk of Sunderland – the supporters – with indifference. Nothing could be further from the truth. Nobody who earns a living in football can ever afford to treat the fans with anything other than deep respect, and not merely for financially selfish reasons. For if it is these fans who pay your wages, it is also they who give the game atmosphere, who can bring out the best – or worst – in a professional footballer.

They are, in an almost literal sense, part of the game itself. And nowhere more so than around the north-east of England. For enthusiasm, the fans of Sunderland, Newcastle and possibly Middlesbrough are equalled only by those in Glasgow and, in more recent times, by those in Liverpool. In the middle 1960s, you could have thrown eleven red-and-white jerseys out on to Roker Park, and 20,000 would have turned up just to have a look at them. Only Manchester United had bigger average crowds, and don't forget that Sunderland were winning no trophies, no titles. These supporters were, and are, fantastic people – like the Scots, they always know a trier when they see one. They respect honesty, because they are themselves honest, decent working-class. Above all, though, they appreciate good football, and I never willingly short-changed them. To do so would have been amateurish. I've been called a few things in my time, but nobody ever called me an amateur.

In fact, if I had to make a choice between the enthusiasm of Rangers and Sunderland fans, I might well have to come down on the side of Sunderland. For one reason: it didn't take as much to please the

Sunderland supporters. At Ibrox, they have no interest in being second-best ... to anybody.

I mentioned never having willingly short-changed the fans. Well, I suppose I should adjust that slightly. At Sunderland I did short-change them ... by being sent off twice. Now I'm not saying that being sent off is unprofessional. Too many very high-class pros have been given the elbow by the referee for such a sweeping statement to make sense. All the same, it is still stupid. That's what you tell yourself afterwards, at any rate. It isn't so easy to be calm and thoughtful when somebody seems to be spending his best energies on cutting you in half. Because of my style, and because of the fact that I was part of the team's 'engine-room', I was the subject of much of that kind of attention. The more I think of it, the more I wonder why I was sent off only twice.

Seriously, I probably deserved both orderings-off. The first was in December 1965 against Nottingham Forest, and I received a 14-day suspension. The second was against Fulham, not long after we had beaten England at Wembley in 1967. I remember the Fulham incident well enough. Mark Pearson, the former Manchester United player, had been having a go at me for most of the game, and I think there were about 20 minutes to go when I lost my head and brought him down in a heap. It wasn't anything like revenge, because I still owed him plenty, but Terry Parmenter, the Fulham captain, reacted as if I'd belted poor wee Pearson with a pick-axe handle. He rushed in and, as the sports writers say, blows were exchanged. I'll say they were. George Kinnell dived in, too, on my side naturally. I could always rely on George. The upshot was that Parmenter was also sent off.

He deserved it. He should have minded his own business. If he had, Fulham just might have saved themselves a point. As it was, we eventually won 3–0, and one of the goals was scored by my old mate and former Ranger, Ralph Brand. The victory helped to soften the blow of my own 'disgrace', for the worst thing about leaving your side with ten men – apart from letting the supporters down – is the possibility that you are taking money out of their pockets. Bonuses are vital to a footballer's wage packet, and don't let anybody ever tell you that ten men are more dangerous than eleven. It's feasible – it has often happened indeed – for ten men to play their hearts out and to survive, maybe win, through sheer guts and physical effort. But in big-time football, especially the English First Division, you should not bet on it. An opposing team of any class can immediately spot the gap, and can usually exploit it.

Inevitably, questions were asked in the Press about whether the second ordering-off was significant – evidence, maybe, that I couldn't quite stand the pace of the First Division. This despite my two years there already! But there's no point in reading too much into the comments of writers who have a column to fill. I'm not criticizing the columnists, who can be entertaining and informative. But, as I say, to worry unduly about what they say can cause genuine depression. Or, the other side of the coin, undeserved elation. Just as an example, consider the opinions of one Scottish writer, the week after I was sent off:

> Baxter could have reached the most crucial time of his career ... recently the storm clouds have hung around the ex-Ranger's tousled head, black and foreboding, on and off the field ... there are rumours that he is unhappy in England ... that the one-time king of Scottish football is only on the fringe of the aristocrats like Alan Ball, Bobby Charlton and Bobby Moore.

On the fringe? That was rich. Only a few months previously, Billy Bremner, Denis Law and I had had the 'aristocrats' running around in ever-decreasing circles, not knowing what day it was.

By contrast, a couple of days later, this appeared in another Scottish newspaper: 'Jim Baxter, though ordered off for the second time in his life last week, is in brilliant form ... playing the best stuff since he went south, Jim has matured considerably and now paces his game perfectly.' See what I mean?

Anyway, I didn't do any more maturing or pacing for 21 days, by courtesy of the F.A. Disciplinary Committee, but I know that my first match on my return was among the best I have ever played. Obviously, this book isn't long enough for me to recount all the good – and bad – games I played, but that one was special, and I hope I'll be forgiven for dwelling on it for a little while. Undoubtedly my suspension had made me doubly eager to get back on the field. There are few things worse than just watching when you *could* be playing, and nothing more frustrating.

The match was against Nottingham Forest, we won 1–0, and the reports the following day were almost embarrassing – yes, even for me, not a man easily embarrassed. Vince Wilson wrote in the *Sunday Mirror*: 'Like a tiger uncaged, Jim Baxter came roaring back . . . in an intensely fought, finely balanced game he was the star, the man of magic who controlled the ball with a superb confidence and an almost blatant cheek. If critics of Jim think they still have a case, I'll change my surname and give a public rendering of Edelweiss.' And Ivor Broadis – who was himself some player in his day – wrote: 'No praise is too great for the foot-fluttering Scot – a veritable dictator among so many soccer serfs.'

That, to be frank, was more or less the general opinion, and if I do make a point of it, it is mainly to indicate how enthusiastic a player can be after a suspension. It proves, I suspect, the old adage about a professional – that he would play for nothing if he had to.

Yet if there is one other club I remember above all from my Roker Park days, that club is Leeds United. Let me add right away that the memories are not pleasant ones. Most people will have their own memories of the Leeds United of the middle to late 1960s – and I cannot doubt that most people will agree with me. Leeds were a nasty lot.

Don Revie, though a friend of mine – we'll just have to

agree to differ now – has a lot to answer for. His team, admittedly, were a poor lot at first. He built them into one of the most successful in the land, but his methods left a lot to be desired. For sheer ruthlessness, there was nobody in their class, nor had there been previously, so far as I know. Certainly there hasn't been anybody since.

All other clubs hated to play Leeds. To them, the rules of the game were a nuisance, merely worth a gesture of lip-service before being ignored. In the art of time-wasting they were the recognized experts. They got up to all sorts of tricks, all sorts of gamesmanship. If you tried to take a free-kick against Leeds just outside their penalty-area, you'd have three or four of them standing on your toes. It wasn't as if they hadn't heard of the ten-yard rule. They simply didn't believe in it . . . either that or they couldn't count.

Most teams, when defending at a corner-kick, are liable to jostle the attacking side. That's par for the course. It is expected, and you take measures against it. But Leeds would be digging away before the ball had even been placed for the kick, and while you were shouting for justice to the referee, their arms would be thrown up in angelic innocence. If they knocked you down and picked you up, they'd pick you up by your hair.

Every one of them could kick, and I don't mean the ball. Even their goalkeepers took the view that attack was the best form of defence in any confrontation. It can be imagined, then, what some of the outfield players were like . . . no, as you were, *all* of the outfield players. A Leeds player, standing on a traffic island, waiting for a bus to pass, would lash out at the bus just for a bit of practice.

Of course, one of the great Leeds players before the title-winning team was built was Bobby Collins. Bobby was a genuine artist on the ball, but he could slice your leg off at the knee and take the bottom bit home before you knew anything about it.

That was the irony of Leeds. Every man could play.

Think of names like Norman Hunter, Paul Madeley, Johnny Giles, Billy Bremner, Jackie Charlton and Mick Jones. They didn't have to be assassins, they didn't have to intimidate. Or did they? Did Don Revie insist on such tactics? Did ruthlessness become an ineradicable habit? I don't know, but I am convinced that the recent decline of Leeds has not aroused a lot of sympathy.

Strangely enough, Sunderland often performed very creditably against Leeds, though one explanation may have been that we had a few players, notably Todd, Kinnell and Brand, who weren't easily intimidated, and who were highly experienced. And of all the many incidents in matches between the two clubs, the one I remember best involved Ralphie Brand.

Brand was no coward, and no great respecter of reputations. After all, he had no mean reputation himself. But, in one drawn game with Leeds, he indulged himself with a couple of sly digs at big Jackie Charlton. Predictably, he chose the wrong man. Jackie looked at him, picked him up, lifted him into the air, and threw him down on the deck. The referee either didn't see anything, or decided that justice had been done.

8

Down in the Forest

If I have given the impression that I was always a favourite with everybody at Roker Park, then I should make a guarded apology. When I first arrived, as I said earlier, it was hard going, and some people expected me to win the League and Cup double for Sunderland in my initial season there.

Things did improve, but not significantly enough. That is not intended to be disrespectful towards some of those who arrived after me. My eventual transfer from Sunderland caused much comment from the fans, and most of it was antagonistic towards the board. My word need not be taken for that. Let me quote from the correspondence pages of the local newspaper, just after I left the north-east.

- I've been a Sunderland fan for years, and I've often been amazed by the comings and goings, but this is the last straw.
- Baxter was an idol at Roker ... he could set a dull game alight. Without him, gates will drop even further.
- The Sunderland board is once again guilty of a colossal blunder. For years, Ian McColl has been trying to build a team, and now he has lost his king-pin.
- Baxter has done a tremendous job at Sunderland ... he was a rock to depend on, when things were going wrong.

These were only a few of the signed letters (complete with addresses) and they gave me heart. I really had done my best at Sunderland, and I know I was appreciated. The club was short of cash, which was why I was sold. But that was not a reason which would placate some of the finest supporters in the world.

In any event, the Sunderland club couldn't have thought too badly of me. When buying me from Rangers, they had paid £80,000, a club record. When Nottingham Forest made inquiries about me, they asked for £100,000. And they got it.

It was on a Monday morning, after I had had a good game, that I got the call to meet Forest officials – the manager Johnny Carey and the chairman Tony Wood. The previous season, 1967–68, Forest had finished second in the League, but they had just lost four in a row, and, worse, hadn't even scored a goal in any of them. They had been knocked out of the Fairs Cup by a team of Swiss part-timers, and their fans were fed up. So the board – or the committee, as I believe it was then – had promised a big signing. The big signing was yours truly.

I had no great objections. On the contrary. It's not easy to object when you're picking up £12,000 as a share of the transfer fee, and when your wages are being increased to £120, from the Roker Park £100. Basic, that was. It was commonplace for league leaders, even then, to pay £100 a point, and the second team to pay, say, £80 a point.

There was another big consideration. I had good reason to believe that the Forest decline was very temporary, because they had some excellent players. How could they not shoot up the league with men like Terry Hennessey, Frank Wignall, Ian Moore and, dare I say it, J.B.?

What I perhaps failed to consider, as I totted up the potential cash to be earned at Nottingham, was an old gentleman usually known as Father Time. The more I think about it, the more I wonder . . . did Sunderland sell me in the nick of time? In the nick of time, that is, for their own sake? Was Ian McColl a much shrewder lad

Back home at Ibrox, talking to the Press. Davie White listens, with an enigmatic smile

Still back home – champagne, the lot. I wish I'd had 100,000 bottles – one for every fan

Outside the pub in Paisley Road – scene of many a good time. Scene of too many good times?

Yes, we do look just a little bit past it, don't we? Sorry about that, Denis!

What a right collection we have here – a so-called veterans' international at Ayr in 1976; (*left to right*) Bertie Auld, George Cohen, Gordon Banks, Billy McNeill, Bobby Charlton, Baxter and Roger Hunt

A picture I'm proud of – I always did love the kids. And I never did mind signing autographs

than he was given credit for? Well, that's possible. But the question itself is impossible to answer. It's like asking what would have happened to Scotland if Bruce had lost Bannockburn. Probably the same as has happened, anyway, come to think of it, but I'm sure you know what I mean.

Nobody can ever say, 'Oh, if only I'd taken that road instead of this one, the world would be so much brighter.' There are too many by-ways off the highroads, distracting, tempting by-ways. But if, as I say, I left Sunderland with the good wishes of the fans ringing in my ears, it must also be said that my move to Nottingham Forest was a disaster. A disaster for them, a disaster for me. And the fault was mine. I would never try to hide that fact. I let Forest down, and I let the Forest supporters down.

It seemed that, quite suddenly, the years of self-indulgence had caught up, and that it was time for the piper to be paid. Could I have had another couple of good seasons at Sunderland? It wasn't as if the north-east didn't have its quota of opportunities to enjoy the good life. Again, an impossible question to answer, and I don't intend to try. But it is hardly deniable that most of the headlines I earned at Nottingham were about various scrapes, fights, getting thrown out of pubs, clubs, etc. Once, I had looked forward eagerly to the Sunday papers. But no longer.

I knew what was happening to me. My confidence was all right, my brain was functioning well enough, but I was losing that crucial yard of pace. I had never been a speed merchant, but at least I had been fast enough to make use of my ball control. All players, no matter how talented, struggle when that happens. Ordinary players can nip in and take the ball away, whereas, with that yard, you'd have left them looking the wrong way.

Training was becoming harder and harder, reminding me of what Dave Mackay used to tell me when I was in my early twenties. On Scotland tours abroad we would normally be allowed to have a good night out after the game, and we would not be asked to train the following morning. (I have seen some sorry sights at many a European breakfast table, let me tell you, and there were plenty of players who never made the breakfast table at all. Quite often I was one of them!) There was never the smallest chance of my training when I wasn't obliged to do so. Dave Mackay had an entirely different outlook. No matter how late Dave stayed up, no matter how much bevy Dave lowered, he was invariably up in time to sweat, training hard, for a full hour.

'Jim,' he would say, almost despairingly, 'what's the matter with you? You think you'll be twenty-three for ever? It doesn't work that way. What's an hour out of your day? What's an hour, when it can be worth years later on? The time will come when you won't be able to train, never forget that.'

'You're right, Dave,' I would say, 'you're right.' But I would still stay in my bed on those Thursday mornings. In my own mind I was quite sure that, yes, of course I would always be twenty-three. But the intervening five years had made one hell of a difference.

It didn't happen immediately. In my very first match at Nottingham, against Sheffield United, I played at least adequately, and we won 2–1. In spite of a bus strike in the city, the crowd was 35,000. At Sunderland, the same afternoon, there was the lowest home gate of the season – 21,189 – against Leeds United.

Which puts me in mind of another match against Leeds, this time for Forest. It was in a late round of the Cup, and we looked like winning a replay on our own ground. Then Jimmy Greenhoff, the Leeds player who went to Manchester United, won a penalty. Only it wasn't a penalty, despite what the referee said. Greenhoff had been harassing our goalkeeper, and I moved in, to lend support. At no time did I touch Greenhoff. But he threw himself in the air, and landed on the deck as if pole-axed. So it was 2–1 for Leeds. Typical of them. No wonder they were hated.

Just about the only headlines I like to remember from

my Forest days were those that appeared on the morning after we beat Liverpool 2–0 at Anfield in the league. The pitch was covered in snow, and I was able to hold and pass the ball almost as well as ever. I wonder how many fixed-odds coupons we ruined that week-end.

Maybe I should be a little kinder to myself, at this point. I'm not saying that I wasn't ever worth my wages at Forest. Had that been the case, they wouldn't have let me play. No, when I talk about the mutual disaster of Forest and myself, it has to be remembered that they paid what was then an enormous fee. For £100,000 I should have done much, much more for them. I should have won games for them, week after week. That's what they deserved, and that's what I couldn't give them. It wouldn't have been so bad if Forest had been a nasty club, like Leeds, or if they'd been run by greedy, grasping people who didn't care about football. But they were really pleasant people, with an honest set-up. Forest were a club to be proud of. There was no niggling, no back-biting, no dressing-room cliques, and no interference from the committee. Also, Nottingham was a good place to live. For me, as I noted, maybe too good.

Johnny Carey, the manager, certainly didn't give me any trouble. Better, I think, if he had done so. He was a manager of the old school, and fast going out of fashion. He stayed in his office. I doubt if we saw him, most weeks, before a quarter-to-three on Saturday afternoons. Tommy Cavanagh was the coach. Tommy, who later joined Tommy Docherty at Manchester United, was always bubbling with enthusiasm, a great motivator as the current jargon has it. He and the Doc were made for each other, I suppose. But Cavanagh, for all his virtues, could hardly be put in the same category as Docherty. He was hardly an original thinker. In general conversation he would say something that sounded quite wise. Then you'd remember that you had heard it before, from someone like Bill Shankly or Joe Mercer. But Cav was still a great lover of the game and, anyway, there wasn't a lot wrong with quoting Shankly or Mercer, even if he didn't acknowledge the source.

If only he hadn't been so crazy on tactics. All the boring new stuff was coming into the game about that time, fancy phrases that were really invented to cover up for mediocre players. And for mediocre coaches, though Cav was better than that.

One instruction really got on my nerves. 'Behind the ball!' It made no sense at all. 'When you lose the ball, get right back, make it hard for them!' Make it hard for *them*? It was hard for everybody, and to what point? What was the point of Frank Wignall or Joe Baker or Ian Moore or Barry Lyon – a fine winger – messing about in their own half, sometimes in their own penalty area? As for me, no wonder I was puffed out.

If you have men who are good at taking on a defence, turning it on the wings, you don't ask them to get in the way of their own defence as soon as they lose possession. If you have men who can score goals – which is still a precious gift – you put them in a position where they can do most damage. Then you get the ball to them. And if your defenders can't cope without the help of your strikers, you get yourself new defenders. As it happened, we had a good solid defence at Forest, but it was too often bemused by 'tactics'.

The stop-watch was coming in then, too. Was this training for the Olympics, I used to think, or was it football? Maybe I do have an axe to grind here, but, while I believe in the importance of fitness, it shouldn't be an obsession. It has its proper place, and I'm not forgetting that I speak as one who didn't always recognize the place. It should never be preached to the detriment of real football. Nobody can run faster than a well-placed pass. And nothing chases the fans away more quickly than teams which rely on running about like bluebottles for 90 minutes. It's not a question of choosing between fitness and ability. Of course, both are necessary. However, leaving my own example out of it, all coaches should remember that although you can often make a talented player very fit, it *never* works the other way round.

At the end of eighteen months came the parting of the ways between Forest and myself. It was not unexpected. I was, in fact, on the transfer list at £15,000, which didn't do my ego very much good. What *was* unexpected was the free transfer.

I read about it first in the newspapers, a fact which, despite my readily-confessed affection for the Nottingham Forest club, I find hard to forgive. I couldn't believe it. I was devastated. How would anybody feel, if he looked casually at the back page of an evening newspaper and read that his employer didn't want him any more? It could be that I deserved a 'free'. But not the way it happened. There was no point, however, in making a big fuss about it. Not when other headlines, also unwanted, were remembered.

It was the spring of 1969. One of the worst moments of my career. It didn't last too long, though. Quite soon, I was on my way home. Home to Ibrox!

9

The homecoming

The shock of being made available on a free transfer by Forest was still painful when I received a call from a journalist friend, Davie Allister of the *Daily Express*, in Glasgow. 'Jim,' he said, 'don't go anywhere before we have a good talk. I wouldn't be surprised if you're back at Ibrox soon.' Well, that, as they say, was a real turn-up for the book. But what a tremendous boost it gave me. Imagine it, to be wanted again by Rangers!

You may have gathered already that I didn't invariably see eye to eye with Rangers. The club had, and has, many faults. But, to me, they were *the* club. So many great times were associated with them, and so many great successes. I think it must be true, the old legend about 'once a Ranger, always a Ranger'. There's just something about the club, about Ibrox, that makes a player walk ten feet tall. And here they were, about to give me a second chance. I didn't really doubt that it would happen, despite the unofficial source. Lots of transfers have been arranged through third parties, and these third parties, more often than not, are trustworthy journalists.

About the same time, by the way, there was another approach, again through a journalist, but this time from Johnny Harvey, the manager of Hearts. This, too, helped to restore my ego, for Hearts are one of the great clubs in Scottish football. But, of course, they weren't Rangers, and that made all the difference. I decided to take Davie Allister's advice, and wait for the call from Ibrox.

Davie Allister, in fact, came down to Nottingham, and, not long after, I was in touch with Davie White, who was then manager of Rangers. The deal was on. I wanted a one-year contract, which I received. It was my idea that, if I did well during that year, I could renegotiate for maybe another two years. Renegotiation, reasonably enough, would have meant more money.

A word now about Davie White. I had a lot of time for the man. I have no doubt he could have grown into the stature of a really good manager for Rangers, but he was never given the opportunity. Influential people always seemed to have the knives out for him.

Willie Waddell and Willie Woodburn, for instance, were former Rangers stalwarts who had played in the so-called 'Iron Curtain' team of the late 1940s, and they couldn't understand how Rangers could have a manager who had never played for the club. That made no sense to me, seeing that Bill Struth, one of the most successful Ibrox managers of all, hadn't even been a footballer. Waddell labelled him 'Boy David' which was grossly unfair. Unless my memory has gone daft, White had lost only one game the previous season, which is some record — even if that defeat was the one that let Celtic in to win the League. He was still crucified, and I think there were two key occasions which, in combination, provided the excuse to get rid of him.

The first was defeat by Celtic in the League Cup. It was in the summer of 1969 that I signed again for Rangers, and the second match I played was against Celtic. We won that one, all right, 2–1 at Ibrox. But they beat us at Parkhead, and went on to qualify at the top of the section. That was the problem, you see. If it had been anybody else but Celtic... Again I'm reminded of how Scot Symon, a man who had done it all at Ibrox, was fired when his team led the League: merely because Celtic were capturing too much limelight in South America playing for the world club championship!

The second turning-point for Davie White was the European Cup Winners' Cup tie against Gornik, a very hard, tough and clever Polish side. We had beaten the Rumanians, Steaua, in the first round, and I did a fair job myself in that tie. Gornik were different, although we could and should have beaten them. What happened *off* the field is a much more unhappy memory for me.

In Poland, Gornik won 3–1. Persson, our Norwegian winger, scored the Rangers goal, but they had one of the finest forwards then playing in Europe, Lubanski. He got two. Even so, we took the view that we could overcome that deficit at Ibrox, and so did most of the Press. European sides don't travel well – especially if they have to travel to places like Ibrox, Parkhead or Liverpool.

As usual, Rangers went down to Largs to train for the second leg. It was an excellent place to relax, away from the pressures – to say nothing of the temptations – of Glasgow, the ticket-hunters, the critics, the hangers-on.

My room-mate was wee Willie Henderson. We were always great friends, appreciating each other's out-going philosophy, and certainly appreciating what we did for each other on the park. I could never count the number of times I've flighted a pass a few yards in front of Willie – who would be going full speed at the time, knowing where the ball would be. Nor could I count the number of times he has put across a perfect ball to Jimmy Millar or Ralph Brand.

Anyway, the night before the game, we took a couple of sleeping-pills. Does that surprise anyone? It shouldn't. Most nights, professional footballers sleep like logs, no bother at all, and without chemical aids. But on the eve of a big European game, the mind is bound to be racing, computing every possibility, playing the 90 minutes in advance. It's not really anxiety, it's more excitement, anticipation. Footballers aren't turnips, despite what some intellectual snobs may think.

We knew what the routine the next day would be. Breakfast about ten o'clock, a loosening-up session, a light lunch (or maybe no lunch at all), bed until about four o'clock, although we wouldn't be sleeping, steak or chicken with salad, and on the road to Glasgow. That, at

THE HOMECOMING

any rate, was what the routine should have been. For Willie Henderson and me, it didn't quite turn out that way.

Let me explain now that, with the possible exception of a coal-face worker on a Monday morning, there's nobody harder to get out of bed than a professional footballer. Ask any coach, any trainer! The knock comes on the door – the coach always seems to get up in good time – and the tradition is to shout several rude words from beneath the snugness of the blankets. There's another tradition. If you do NOT get up fairly smartly after that, you're liable to be the unwilling recipient of a cup of cold water. It's all a bit of a laugh, in a way, and is part and parcel of the procedure when footballers are living away from home.

Laurie Smith, the Rangers physiotherapist, presumably was in no mood for a laugh. It was Smith who knocked at our door. 'All right, all right,' we bawled, 'give us peace, we'll be down, in a minute.'

I guarantee that not more than 20 minutes had passed when I said to Willie: 'Come on, wee man, better get some breakfast.' We had had no reminder. We were entitled to think we had ample time. Down we went to the breakfast room. We looked around. It was about ten o'clock. And there wasn't a soul in the place. I asked a hotel porter: 'What's going on here? Where's the team?.' Away training, I was told.

We couldn't believe our ears. Were we outcasts or something? Could nobody have bothered to give us another warning – or even to come into the room and throw water over us? It was as if there was some conspiracy . . . to get on the bus to training *before* Baxter and Henderson came down. Almost a deliberate ploy. I still don't know the truth of it or, at least, of the motives behind it. But it was obvious that Smith had persuaded Davie White to make examples of us, as if we were cheeky schoolboys.

That wasn't nearly the worst, however. Having no transport, we couldn't join the team for training, whether we were late or not, so we had to cool our heels until they all came back to the hotel. Davie White steamed straight into us. We told him exactly what had happened. But the next thing we knew, sports reporters were down from Glasgow. They had heard all sorts of tales. Baxter and Henderson had been seen the night before at a Glasgow casino. Baxter and Henderson had been at parties in Largs.

I swear there wasn't a word of truth in it, and, considering that I have hidden little else in this book, I am entitled to be believed. How do these stories get around, anyway? I wish I knew. When Davie White confronted us with lying accusations, our only reaction was unbelieving shock. As we told him, we had both done some daft things in our time, but we weren't *that* daft.

I'm pretty sure Davie did believe us, but, if only for the fact that we had missed training, he had to do something. So at about half-past-one there we were, going through a two-man training session right in front of the hotel, and with the Press watching. It was humiliating. Cheeky schoolboys? We felt like convicts on punishment detail.

The irony was this: although Willie and I were the two best players for Rangers that night – and that's not only my opinion – we had to carry much of the responsibility for another defeat by Gornik. And by the same score, 3–1.

I got a goal early in the game – I think I scored with the right foot, believe it or not – and we dominated the game for long periods. But the pressure came to nothing, through no fault of Willie Henderson, who played his heart out. They broke away just about on the hour, and Olek equalized. That really gave them confidence, and Lubanski took our whole defence on before making it 2–1. Their sub got the third and, quite frankly, we just about deserved the 6–2 thrashing on aggregate. Perhaps we hadn't had a lot of luck, but that would be a poor excuse. The Poles were a better side. In fact they reached the final of the Cup Winners' Cup, only to be beaten by Manchester City.

It didn't matter, however, that Willie and I had played well. The only talk was of a party that never took place – just as if we had both played stinkers through lack of sleep and too much booze. What could be more ironic than the fact that, after all the parties I had been at, after all the wild nights I'd had, I took most stick for something that was *supposed* to have happened at a time when I was tucked up in bed with a sleeping-pill.

The Gornik result saw Davie White out of the door at Ibrox. Sadly, he also had to take some of the blame for the fictional antics of Baxter and Henderson. Why hadn't he kept us under control? Why hadn't he checked that we were in bed? Nobody asked why he hadn't put a guard on the door, equipped with machine-gun and Dobermann pinscher, but that was only because nobody thought of it. It was obvious that he just wasn't big enough for the job, wasn't it? That's what his critics implied so heavily, and that's what the Ibrox board acted upon.

And so Willie Waddell took over as manager. He had been manager of Kilmarnock when the Ayrshire club had won the League some years earlier and, in between times, had been writing for the *Daily Express*.

Footballers cannot afford to worry too much about changes of managers. Possibly it's like journalists and editors. The bosses come and go. The workers try to keep their heads down, and earn their wages, while they 'suss out' the new man in control.

I found Willie Waddell a difficult man to understand. In his sports-writing days, he never missed a chance to praise me to the skies. If he did venture some mild criticism – and that was very rarely – you could almost visualize him typing away at his desk with gloomy reluctance. Let me indulge myself with the following quote from Willie Waddell, in the days when he was a gentleman of the Fourth Estate:

'A Scotland team without Baxter strikes me as ridiculous . . . half-fit, he'd be good enough for nine Englishman . . . Baxter is one of the all-time Scottish greats.' So I shouldn't be blamed for having thought that, at the very least, the new manager of Rangers would be cordial towards me.

I played one first-team match for Rangers under Waddell. That was against Aberdeen, when I was injured. It was also my last first-team game. But that's no more than a statistic. What really baffled me about Waddell was the way he avoided me at Ibrox. Why? Goodness knows. But he did. Was it embarrassment, a guilty conscience, or what? What did he have to be embarrassed about? What could he have to feel guilty about? He had helped, as a journalist, to put the boot into Davie White, the man who brought me back to Rangers, but that explained nothing.

If I was about to go up the marble staircase at Ibrox, and he was about to go down, he would go back into his office, clearly to avoid the obligation of conversation, however brief. That kind of incident was repeated, more or less, on many occasions. I have only a tiny germ of suspicion as to why he acted the way he did. It can be no more than that. Was he planning to get rid of me as soon as he took over?

Whether that's the case or not, it was in January 1970 that I heard on the grape-vine that I was in line for a free transfer from Rangers. The grape-vine was accurate. It usually is. When I was eventually called up to the manager's office, I was under no illusions. Baxter was for the chop again. I remember that day only too clearly.

I met big Dave Provan on his way down the stairs. He was trying to hold back the tears. Davie was a ferociously loyal Ranger, and he had been given the treatment that was about to be my own lot. I tried to cheer him up, but I don't think I succeeded. I'll never understand why Rangers don't make *some* attempt to give jobs to ex-players who have proved their loyalty. Men like Provan, Jimmy Millar, Bobby Shearer, Davie Wilson, Eric Caldow, Ralph Brand ... they would have given any-thing to stay on at Ibrox in some capacity. Of course, not all can be taken on. But why so pathetically few? Why

THE HOMECOMING

this determination to dump good servants as soon as they can't play so well any more?

Meanwhile, Willie Waddell and his assistant, Willie Thornton – well, they, at least, were former Rangers – were waiting for me. They sat behind their desks. I thought of how often I had gone into that manager's office, on very different business, and in a very different capacity. I thought of how often I had been received as a favourite son by Scot Symon. But I didn't start feeling sorry for myself.

I got the impression that Waddell and Thornton were expecting me to explode, to tell them what a right pair they were, and in no uncertain language. I had no intention of doing any such thing. Predictably, Willie Waddell did the talking. 'Well, Jim, this is sorry news I have for you, but I have to tell you that the Rangers Football Club no longer requires your services. I want to thank you now for all you have done for the club.' Big deal!

I simply said they had a heavy job on their hands, and wished them and Rangers the best of luck. 'See you some time,' I said, and walked out. A couple of weeks later, Waddell phoned me and confirmed that he had indeed been waiting for me to start shouting about injustice and ingratitude. He should have known me better than that.

It's hardly a happy memory, though. I had returned to Rangers, eager to erase from my own and from the public mind any hint of the reputation I had gained at Nottingham. I was willing and able to train, and I know I played some good stuff. But maybe, just maybe, my return was a mistake. The fans were looking for the Jim Baxter of old, and there was no such person. Also, the team of 1969–70 was nowhere near the calibre of the one I had left. Again, that's not an excuse. It's the truth, as any Rangers fan will agree. So I was expected to be the king again, and it couldn't be done.

'Never go back,' somebody once said. He could have been right.

10

The great ones

Anybody who gives an opinion on the ten or twenty best footballers ever risks obvious argument. Well, I've never shirked an argument in my life. The opinions in this chapter are based on what I have seen, but there is more to it than that.

When you talk about the best footballers, what do you really mean? Do you mean the most effective? Kevin Keegan would probably be in that class, and so would most of the England World Cup side of 1966. Or do you mean those you enjoyed watching above all others? Those with that extra special spark, that inborn gift which is a special category of the world-class player.

Surely everything must depend on what you yourself think of football as a game? If you're happy to see a boring team win, then we're not talking the same language. Nobody questions the importance of winning. But anybody who questions the importance of winning with style – and maybe joy – would be more at home watching the heavy events at an athletics meeting.

Nobody gave me more joy than George Best. Even playing against him, I could appreciate the man's genius. He was the finest footballer I ever saw, and I include Pele in that summing-up. Naturally, I would never criticize Pele. I didn't see him often enough – although I did play against him once, and I remember with justifiable pride that he said, afterwards, that he wished I had been born a Brazilian. That was some compliment. And yet Best remains for me the best.

There was no football virtue he didn't have. Before somebody mentions height, let me say that George didn't have to be tall. He could jump higher than most six-footers. And you couldn't frighten him. Plenty tried. He used to be kicked all over the park. When he was younger, he would just get up – if he could – shrug his shoulders, and get on with tormenting the opposition. Similar to Willie Henderson, in that respect. When he grew a little older, and started getting bruises on the bruises, his temper grew shorter. Can you blame him?

Maybe I should declare a personal interest now. Most of the players I include in my very top category were like myself in a way. They hated training, and they were not averse to a wild night. At training, they would do only what they had to do. If they had trained harder, they might have played for longer. But if they had had a dedicated attitude towards training, they would have been different people, possibly lesser players. To me, that's a fair point. I would never discount what goes on in a player's mind. Natural talent and arrogance can often go together – and blend sweetly.

Charlie Cooke, of Aberdeen and Chelsea, didn't enjoy training, but I never saw anybody who could match Charlie for pure ball-control. Once, when he was playing for Aberdeen against Rangers, he made a terrible mess of Ronnie McKinnon. Four times he showed Ronnie the ball, with his foot on top of it, and four times he conjured it away from him. Now you see it, now you don't. I almost begged Scot Symon to sign him, and I'm still not sure what went wrong. Perhaps Charlie preferred the lights of London to Glasgow; or perhaps he was beginning to develop the reputation of a hell-raiser which, if true, would have put Mr Symon right off. With Cooke and Baxter in the same team, Scot wouldn't have had a moment's peace.

It was in 1966, at Largs, that Charlie and I should have looked ahead and predicted the results of our dislike of training. The Scotland squad was preparing for a friendly against Portugal, and there was the usual curfew. We went out on the town, if you can use that phrase about Largs. It's not exactly Las Vegas. However, we found a fair quota of amusement, and we didn't get back until four in the morning.

Walter MacCrae, the trainer, a fearsome sergeant-major of a man, saw us stagger in. 'We'll see you in the morning,' he said. And in the morning the two of us were taken aside. 'Okay,' said Walter, 'so you think you can do your job, whatever you've done the night before. Let's see if that's true.' He took out his stop-watch and set a series of punishing exercises. Within five minutes we were as sick as dogs. Yes, that should have been the warning sign!

Jimmy Greaves often tells viewers that training was always, for him, a nuisance. In his case, maybe it was. Jimmy never ran about, unless he had the ball near goal. Then he would stick it into the back of the net. There was never a player born who could score goals like Jimmy Greaves – I make no apologies for repeating myself. When he had the goal in his sights, it didn't matter a lot how many players were in front of him – two, three or nobody but the goalie. And it should be noted that many a centre-forward fails when he has only the keeper to beat, because he can't stand the pressure of having no excuse if he misses. Greaves never needed any excuses for anything. It was a question of 'Where d'you want it, left, right, or between the goalie's legs?' He made the choice, just like he was choosing between a tuppeny ice-cream wafer or a threepenny one.

Willie Hamilton is a name which will be unfamiliar to many readers, and that's a shame. He died before he was 40, for he was never a healthy man, but he was a beautiful footballer. Apart from his attitude to training, Willie was also like myself in his attitude to the ball. That is, if you didn't have the ball, you were wasting your time. We hated belting up and down the field, so we didn't. But when we got the ball, we could do something with it. 'Otherwise,' somebody once wrote, 'we were like Menuhin minus the violin.' I quite like that.

Jock Stein is on record as saying that Willie Hamilton is his choice as the best of all. Well, Jock has never been one of my favourite people, to be honest, and I wouldn't be surprised if the feeling is mutual. He has always struck me as somebody who likes you to think he knows everything about you, including things that are none of his business. But if he chooses Willie Hamilton as his No. 1, I'm not arguing.

Peter Osgood was a man who actually aroused my envy, and that's not easy for me to say. At the age of 20, he looked like an Adonis, big, strong, with a bearing that was almost military. And what a player! For all his size, he had grace, combined with the balance of a ballet-dancer. He was another I could watch with genuine pleasure, because his gifts were so clearly natural. In every sense of the word, Peter had class.

Jimmy Johnstone and Bobby Murdoch must be mentioned, and it's reasonable to do so in the same sentence. They played together like a dream, and yet they were so different. Then again, maybe the blend was so good *because* they were so different.

Bobby tackled like a bear, and passed the long ball immaculately, but that's not why I include him in my élite category. No, it's because he, too, had style. Unmistakeably so. He was the most important player in the Celtic side which won the European Cup, and there was a lot of competition for that accolade.

From wee Johnstone, for example, who could beat as many players as you put in front of him. No wonder they called him 'Jinky'. He turned and twisted like the proverbial eel. Possibly he made himself dizzy at times, but not before he had terrorized just about every defender in sight. What he did to poor Terry Cooper in the semi-final of the European Cup against Leeds in 1970 should have been prohibited by Act of Parliament.

Alan Hudson, Alfredo di Stefano and Ferenc Puskas cannot be left out of any list of players blessed with God-given talent. But it won't have escaped your notice that I'm having to go back a bit in time. That's not nostalgia.

It's an honest appraisal.

From the 1980s, who can compare with the above names? Kevin Keegan has been called the best footballer in Britain – some have said in Europe – and if that is so, then I have to worry for the cause of football. This is not Keegan's fault. I have never met him, but I admire his determination and the way he has obviously worked to iron out natural deficiencies. Also he has more natural skill than he is often given credit for.

The fault lies with those who have substituted tactics for talent. Or, to put it another way, with those coaches and managers who, having minimum talent at their disposal, have concentrated on tactics to compensate. The inevitable outcome has been the discouragement of the naturally gifted player. Indeed, this kind of player is not only discouraged but also distrusted.

When England won the World Cup in 1966, it was assumed, by those who didn't understand real football, that they had a lot of good players. Well, perhaps they did have *good* players, but how many great ones? One for sure, two arguably. Gordon Banks has to be among the best goalkeepers of all time, and you can go back to Jerry Dawson and John Thomson, if you like. Bobby Moore was highly talented, but we weren't permitted to see his ultimate potential – if, that is, it was any more than the obvious. Sir Alf Ramsey wanted the game played in zones, and when did Moore move out of his allotted territory? He did the job he had to do brilliantly. But if it wasn't much of a job, it wasn't his fault.

The full-backs could tackle and attack, in accordance with the Ramsey dictum which excluded orthodox wingers. As I also mention elsewhere, Jackie Charlton was a fair enough footballer, but nobody ever accused him of finesse. Nobby Stiles should never have been allowed to play for England. He had no class whatever, and no pretensions to class. Alan Ball had a certain demented efficiency, but was easily fooled, while Hurst and Hunt were hardly better than labourers. Peters was a bit better than a labourer, but did anybody ever get a tingle of anticipation when he was on the ball?

That leaves Bobby Charlton, who is apparently something of a legend. I have never been sure why. He is a pleasant, courteous man, but his main characteristic on the field was scoring from about half-a-mile out. This he persisted in trying to do, with a tiny success rate. His goals were remembered. People like Paddy Crerand and Denis Law remember, with frustration, the countless times he missed. Still a good player though.

No doubt, I will be accused of impertinence because of the way I have dismissed a team which won the World Cup. Well, that team epitomizes my point. It played pedestrian rubbish, and it won. These things can happen. But can anyone with any feeling for the game compare that unfortunately much-copied England side with *any* Brazil team, with the Dutch of 1974, with the Hungarians of 1954, or even with the Argentinians of 1966 or 1978?

Anyway, having tried to demolish one myth, let me have a go at another. You will have heard of the great Rangers 'Iron Curtain' side of the late 1940s. It was supposed to be invincible when the heavy grounds found out those sides with less stamina. All because of the ferocious training standards at Ibrox, so it is said. Yes, well, that's not what I heard from Ian McColl, who was a member of the 'Iron Curtain' invincibles.

The trainer at the time was Jimmy Smith, and Jimmy had a dog called, say, Bonzo. One name is as good as any. Jimmy would set a training schedule for stalwarts such as George Young, McColl, Willie Waddell, Willie Woodburn, Willie Thornton and (probably the ringleader) Sammy Cox. Then Jimmy would retire to the trainer's room with his pipe and the newspapers. The above mentioned crew would sit on their backsides behind one of the goals, several of them puffing contentedly at non-filter fags. Then they would throw some water on their faces, practise heavy breathing, and report to Jimmy.

'Bonzo,' Jimmy would say to the dog, 'did they do their training? Did they do the 40 laps, and the dozen sprints?' Depending on whether or not Bonzo wagged his tail, Jimmy would call it a day, or order the lads out for another session which they also ignored. Now I have to be fair. I'm not saying – nor did Ian McColl – that this was the regular idea of training at Ibrox. But it does indicate how myths can develop, doesn't it?

I like to think it's all true. It is exactly what I'd have done myself, given the chance.

11

Golden Millar

Of all the players I ever knew, there was none more honest than Jimmy Millar. For every pound he was paid, Jimmy always gave a pound's worth of effort, and then a bit more on top. And as I've stressed elsewhere, he wasn't just a 100 per cent trier. As a centre-foward, he had plenty of class.

But I have to say that there were times when Jimmy's honesty and sheer integrity could be somewhat frustrating. I recall in particular the European tie with Munchengladbach in the early sixties. We won 11–1 on aggregate, not a bad result for Rangers against what was supposed to be one of the best sides in Germany.

It was the usual routine on the trip over there. We arrived on the Monday for the match on the Wednesday, and that evening we were allowed to stroll around the town, to stretch our legs. That wasn't too exciting and at about half-past-ten in the evening I was in a pleasant little bar, sipping a beer in the company of Jimmy Millar and another colleague. Sipping beer wasn't too exciting, either, but a couple of girls at the bar seemed to have a lot of potential. I couldn't speak a word of German, except 'Ja' or 'Nein', but I strolled across and soon made myself understood. Returning to our table, I gave them the news. 'No bother,' I said. 'They've got a mate, we're all fixed up.'

Jimmy wouldn't consider it. 'No chance. I'm having nothing to do with them. Anyway, there's an eleven o'clock curfew, and that's when I'll be back, and not a minute later. For God's sake, Stanley, we've got a match on Wednesday. Behave yourself.' Stanley was my nickname, for obvious reasons.

Nothing I said could budge him. 'Look,' I said, 'we'll be back by half-past-twelve or so, we'll say we got lost, no problem. You said yourself, we're not playing till Wednesday.'

Jimmy just shook his head.

'I know what's wrong with you,' I said. 'You're flapping.'

He went wild. He was over the table, and he had me by the throat. A very strong lad was Jimmy, I can tell you. 'Flapping, am I? Flapping? I'll screw your head off.' For a few seconds, I thought he meant exactly that, but the third member of our party managed to pull him off. He stormed out, still blazing mad.

'What the hell was that about?' I asked, my tie down the back of my neck.

I was to find out the next morning, when Jimmy came over to apologize, and that, too, shows the kind of man he was. When I said that he was 'flapping', I only meant that he was running scared, and he should have known that nobody would ever have seriously accused him of cowardice. But, by accident, I had used exactly the word calculated to madden him. Jimmy, for all his speed and skill on the football park, did tend to walk like a penguin, and constant jibes – usually from very big centre-halves – had made him extremely sensitive. 'Flapper' was a nickname he detested almost as much as he detested 'Penguin feet'.

You may be sure that I learned from that mistake. I didn't want to spend the rest of my life walking one way and looking the other.

Jimmy Millar also figures largely in one of the most notorious games ever played by Rangers in Europe. Which Rangers fan will forget the 'Barbars of Seville'? It was the European Cup Winners' Cup, and the return leg in Seville on 26 September 1962, was the worst I have ever been in. If we weren't afraid for our lives, we were certainly afraid of the real prospect of permanent injury.

We were at our very best in the first leg, winning 4–0. Seville were out-classed, and they knew it. There was one player who did nothing except sneer at us and say things like: 'Baxter, in Seville . . .' And he would make a throat-cutting movement. He issued similar threats to every Rangers player who would listen to him. When that second leg started over there, he was almost as good as his word. He had no knife, so far as I could see, but I was expecting him to take one out of his stocking any minute. His mates were no better.

They had no chance of taking the tie, so they tried to put us out of the *next* round, by other means. There was no attempt on their part to play football. They just whacked us, no matter where the ball was, and usually they sneaked up from behind. They had been yellow at Ibrox, and weren't much better at home, but were bolstered by the home fans, who had presumably strayed from the bull-ring. The referee, meanwhile, simply didn't want to know. Everywhere he looked there were people lying on the deck, or fighting, but he carried on as if it was the Salvatian Army versus the Band of Hope.

As the proceedings wore on – I won't call it a game – Rangers were giving as good as they got, having no choice. It was self-defence, and sometimes we retaliated first, knowing that if we didn't, it was a boot stroked down the back of the leg, or right across the shin-bone, or maybe the back of the neck, depending on what was handy at the time.

Then suddenly, there was an incident involving John Greig, a youngster at the time. Jimmy Millar obviously spotted who had got John, and went into the fray enthusiastically on his mate's behalf.

By now, of course, the minutes were ticking away, we were 4–2 up on aggregate and Seville seemed to know they were out. They didn't accept it, though.

The Greig-Millar incident was the final flashpoint. All pretence at playing football vanished. Harold Davis was thumping every Spaniard in sight, and when Harry thumped them, they knew all about it. He had good reason. Some of us were surrounded on the touchline and it was a regular Donnybrook. I was kicked and punched on the head, and spitting blood in more ways than one. Doug Baillie was in the dug-out officially, but he came onto the field to join in, and he could handle himself well.

Over on the other side of the park, I saw one of the Seville players chasing wee Willie Henderson all over the place. He had avoided both Davis and Baillie, and Henderson, presumably, seemed small enough to merit his attention. Anyway, Willie scampered round Willie Ritchie and the Spaniard, with unusual courage, punched Ritchie instead.

I didn't see a great deal more than that because we were still too busy defending ourselves. At some stage the final whistle must have gone, although that is a misnomer. We heard later that the referee had blown early, and the police intervened – late. The police, in fact, escorted us to the dressing-room, which was just as well.

Anyway, in the dressing-room we counted heads, just to make sure that nobody was still lying out there. That was when somebody mentioned the banquet.

The reaction was immediate and unanimous. The Spaniards could stuff their banquet. Imagine sitting down at the same table with a bunch of goons who couldn't play and who had been earnestly trying to put the lot of us in hospital

Enter Scot Symon – and I cannot emphasize too often or too heavily how much of a gentleman he was. 'What's this? We won't go to the banquet? Who's through to the next round of the European Cup Winners' Cup? Glasgow Rangers. Oh yes, we will go to the banquet. We will go as winners.' He was taking it for granted, of course, that, even if the referee had finished the game a little early, there would be no argument about the result and he was proved quite correct. And when Scot talked like that, there was no scope for argument. We went to the banquet.

At the same table as myself there sat Alex Scott, Ralph Brand and another Rangers player who I will call Hamish. That was not his name but he might be embarrassed by public knowledge of what happened next.

We were going well with the wine on the table, and the Bacardi under it, when Alex Scott turned to me and said: 'See Hamish – there's going to be trouble here.' It seemed a fair prediction.

Hamish had never been much of a boozer. He liked a drink but, not being used to the stuff, he would feel the effects very quickly. He leaned over to me: 'When that centre-half goes to the toilet,' he said carefully, 'I'm having him.'

This did not seem like a good idea to me. The Seville centre-half had, admittedly, been one of the worst of the villains but he was built like the lad with the iron teeth in the James Bond film. About ten minutes passed and the Cuba Libres were coming up faster than ever, when the centre-half at last rose and headed for the toilet. So did Hamish.

The three of us thought we should follow and we did, but we were too late. Hamish was already on top of the Spaniard punching the daylights out of him. In fact, the Spaniard was shouting for mercy, or that's what it sounded like. A gentle enough person was Hamish, until you tried to take liberties with him. Incidentally, I have no reason to suppose he has changed.

12

The world's a stage

Wembley has usually been a place of happy memories for me, because we kept on winning there. Well, we won twice there, anyway, when I was in a Scotland jersey, and that will do for now.

And so, on 23 October, 1963, I should have built up the finest memories of all. On that day, I played for the Rest of the World against England in the Football Association's Centenary International.

By any normal measure, it would be difficult to think of a greater honour. Football is a team game, of course, and in that respect the World Cup Final has to be No. 1. But, in individual terms, selection for a World XI has to come out on top.

Three Scots were on the FIFA short-list, announced earlier that month. Dave Mackay of Tottenham, Denis Law of Manchester United, and myself. I was the only home Scot, and, in the event, Dave Mackay was left out of the final squad. Now that I couldn't understand. I knew there were some very fair half-backs around, between Rio and Vladivostock, but there was not one, in my mind, with the power, skill and leadership qualities of Dave Mackay. Still, there was nothing I could do about that. I had to take the view that, well, you must be able to play a bit, young Baxter, if you're selected from a FIFA set-up of more than 100 countries.

The company was quite something. How many will remember the final 16? Yashin (Russia), Soskic (Yugoslavia): Santos (Brazil), Eyzaguirre (Chile), Schnellinger

(West Germany); Pluskal, Popluhar and Masopust (Czechoslovakia), Baxter (Scotland); Kopa (France), Seeler (Germany), Law (Scotland), Di Stefano (Spain), Eusebio (Portugal), Puskas (Spain), Gento (Spain).

Consider the established names there. Yashin of Russia, that incredible goalkeeper whose arms seemed to be made from elastic. Schnellinger of West Germany, one of the best full-backs I have ever seen. All those Czechs, who had only scrambled past Scotland in a World Cup qualifying group the previous year – but who had gone on to reach the Final itself in Santiago. And look at the forwards. Did you ever see a line-up like it, anywhere, anytime?

I have been asked since if I ever felt just the tiniest twinge of anxiety, as I studied the list of my Rest of the World colleagues. I did not. That year I was at the very peak of form, if not of experience, and all I wanted to do was to show how much I deserved my selection.

The first half was terrible. It was terrible because I wasn't playing. The football was all right, I suppose, but only for the spectators, and I certainly didn't regard myself as a spectator. If I hadn't been called on for the second half, I suspect I'd have done one of two things. I would either have made tracks for the nearest boozer. Or I would have walked onto the park, anyway, and let somebody else go off. But I was chosen to have a go, and I can never forget what was almost my first touch of the ball.

In possession just on the half-way line, I sent a nice one to Puskas, who wasn't well marked. Now that wee Hungarian wrote the book when it came to turning quickly on the ball and shooting. Billy Wright, who tried to play against him when the Hungarians whacked England in 1953, would not argue about that.

This time, Puskas took the pass well, as he should have done, turned, and rattled the ball against the cross-bar. This didn't please me at all. I had given him every chance, and what had he done with it? Wasted it! What was worse, he seemed to be quite pleased with himself, as if he had done something clever. Perhaps I overstated my case when I glared at him and spread out my hands as if to say, 'What more do you want?' but the gesture at least was in keeping with the general atmosphere. That is why I have no specially fond memories of 23 October, 1963.

Nobody wanted to play for the team. They wanted to play only for themselves, to show how clever they were. If that sounds cheeky, coming from me, I would say that – no matter my so-called arrogance – I always tried to keep team-mates supplied with the ball, whether with Raith or with Rangers or indeed anybody else. But that night, on the world's stage, the occasion was interpreted as a chance to strut around doing party-tricks. Denis Law was a predictable exception, and I certainly except myself too. We *were* playing England, after all, and *they* weren't messing about. They wanted to win, as they did, 2–1.

They had no right to win. Had the Rest of the World played like a real team for ten minutes, we could have scored two or three – and *then* we could have played about a bit. But no, Puskas was a pain, holding the ball until somebody took it from him. Di Stefano, an unquestioned genius as a footballer, was no better, and Gento obviously wanted to take the ball home with him. Even Schnellinger was trying to beat England forwards. Often he succeeded, to be fair, but when he did get rid of the ball, we were usually marked off the field.

In a really competitive match, my job would be to give the ball to a forward in a potentially dangerous position – or to anybody who could give me the return, by which time, I would usually have found a space in the opposing defence. In the Centenary match, that was a total waste of time. If I passed to anybody but Law, that would be my last touch for ages. No wonder it was Denis who scored our goal. It was not a state of affairs I accepted with either humility or indifference. I made my opinions very well known, but half of them couldn't speak English and, if they could, pretended to misunderstand.

I think I had a reasonably good game, in spite of it all, but it was no thanks to my alleged team-mates. I learned a lesson, though.

The following year, as I recall, I played for a special select team against England in a testimonial match at Stoke for Sir Stanley Matthews. In the same team were Willie Henderson and . . . Ferenc Puskas. (I hope, by the way, that nobody thinks Puskas and I didn't get on. That's disproved later on in this book. It was on the field, in this kind of game, that friendship was tested and found wanting.)

If Puskas had wanted to be a one-man band at Wembley, he wanted to be a one-man orchestra (and conductor) at Stoke. He began by taking every free-kick, dashing all over the place, positively demanding passes. Soon he was taking throw-ins, when he could, and then he was onto the corner-kicks. I was expecting him to take a corner-kick and beat the ball into the middle, to head it in.

Willie Henderson was as frustrated as I was, but I did something about it. Puskas was about to take yet another free-kick, not in a position where I would normally have taken it. But I'd had enough. I pushed him out of the way. 'Ferenc,' I said, 'Piss off,' more or less. His lack of English, combined with my strong Fife accent, didn't matter. He got the message, and from that point we enjoyed the game.

I took my share of free-kicks, and also took care to see that they went to Henderson and not Puskas. Don't ask me what the final score was. Unless I am permitted to reply: 'Puskas 7, Baxter 8.' Free-kicks, of course.

13

Girls galore

The life of a professional footballer isn't all glamour, but it does have plenty of compensations. The phrase 'groupie' hadn't been invented, so far as I recall, in the early 1960s, but the name of the game was still the same. There were always plenty of girls.

If you were a footballer, and if you didn't have two heads and a hump-back, you were favourite. I'm not sure why that should be, but I can tell you I wasn't asking any questions. I was happy to appreciate my good luck. Maybe it was being in the public eye, in the headlines. Maybe girls liked to be seen out with somebody who was well known. In any event, when I was in my teens and playing for Raith Rovers, I did have a few bob to spare, I *was* well enough known – around Cowdenbeath, that is – and there were no problems, especially at the local Palais dance-hall.

That was the place, then. It's probably a bingo-hall now. Some nights, I would even go with my pals over to Edinburgh to see what the talent was like in the old capital city. It was highly acceptable. Once when we went there, I wore my new genuine Teddy-boy suit. Well, I had always wanted one and where else to go, sporting my pride and joy, but Edinburgh? My mother didn't like it, but she wasn't the boss *all* the time.

We chose a dance-hall called Fairleys, near the top of Leith Street. It had a wild reputation, but that didn't worry us. We were miners from Fife and we could handle ourselves all right. So we thought.

I'm not sure how the fight started. We had had a few drinks, and I wouldn't be surprised if we had been pressing our attentions on ladies already well spoken for. There were stairs going from street-level up to the dance-hall. I must have hit every one of them on the way out. And there I was trying to stand in Leith Street, one shoe missing, a front tooth broken, my nose squashed slightly, and my suit all torn. Seconds later, I was joined on the pavement by my mates, who were in a similar state.

That was one of the first hard lessons I learned, in the matter of birds and booze. Or, to put it more accurately, one of the first hard lessons I ought to have learned. That's funny, I said to myself, dabbing at my bloody nose, and wondering how much a new pair of shoes would cost. I'd always thought that if you had a Teddy-boy suit, you were a hard man. Nobody told me you had to be able to fight. My Teddy-boy days lasted for a month. That suit was flung away. My mother didn't say 'I told you, didn't I?'. But I wouldn't have blamed her if she had done.

Clothes were important to me, I admit it. And it was again in Edinburgh that I did learn a lesson about clothes. Still with Raith Rovers, I was chosen for an Under-23 game, and I was determined to be your regular Beau Brummel. This time I paid top price for a Lovat green suit. I remember admiring myself in the mirror at home in Fife, before catching the train across the Forth. 'Yes, James,' I said, 'you'll do. Not bad at all.'

Next stop was the North British hotel in Princes Street, where the squad was to assemble. I strolled into the main foyer, feeling like David Niven at the Waldorf Astoria. Some of the other players were already there. George Thomson of Hearts, Davie Wilson of Rangers, Alex Young of Hearts and John Baxter of Hibs. I looked at their suits, the finest of mohair, the very latest in fashion, and I felt like changing my mind about playing for the Under-23s. Talk about the hick from the sticks!

Some Press photographers came along later and, no

kidding, I didn't want anything to do with them. I pretended it was shyness. It was nothing of the kind. I just didn't want to be seen, by more people than necessary, in that Lovat green suit.

But as I say, that *was* a lesson learned. Shortly afterwards I moved to Ibrox, and my mind was made up. Keep a low profile for a few months, Baxter, I told myself. See how the land lies. Don't be cheeky. Not yet. Which is exactly what I did. And after about a year, if Glasgow didn't belong to me, I felt as if it did. I could do no wrong. It became crystal clear to me that this was the life I had been born for, and I was enjoying every minute of it. As another song goes, they can't take that away from me.

My old pals from Fife would come over quite regularly, and we'd go to all the best night-spots. The best that we knew, anyway. My picture was in the papers almost every day, and if they weren't calling me a super-star, they were calling me a playboy. I didn't much mind either, to be honest. And my mates couldn't believe their luck. Their eyes would pop almost out of their heads, as we walked into, say, La Ronde in Sauchiehall Street, where good-looking birds were wall to wall. 'Take it easy,' I'd say, real man of the world stuff. 'Don't chase them. They'll be over.' And they were.

Of course, I was still learning. At 21 I didn't know much about anything. The 21-year-olds of today are far more mature. I was still more of a boy than a man. So far as food was concerned, fish and chips or steak and eggs were all right with me, and table-wine was a closed book. There weren't too many restaurants in Cowdenbeath where you could ask for the claret to be served at room temperature, please.

I don't suppose I had progressed far beyond the stage at which Bert Herdman, the Raith Rovers manager, had once told us we could go à la carte, by way of a winning bonus. That's great, we said, at the time. But what's à la carte. Luckily, I was a good learner. I'd listen when a meal was being ordered by somebody who knew what

Baxter on the right – how did you guess – putting away a nice wee pass with the left peg. I can't be sure that Jimmy Millar scored with it, but who wants a bet?

Nottingham Forest, with JB top right. A fine club, a fine bunch of team-mates. I only wish I could have done more for them

Peter Osgood – one of the few I used to envy

Charlie Cooke – sheer class, the man I tried to persuade Rangers to sign

Pele – he said he wished I had been born a Brazilian. A man of good judgement!

Ferenc Puskas – he liked his whisky, and more besides, but what a player!

EAT ONES

George Best – quite simply, the best

Billy Bremner – you always wanted him on the same side. Shame he had to play for Leeds

A terrible pitch, I suppose, but I never really disliked the mud. Here's JB putting away a pass for Sunderland

The Sunderland team that had many of the greatest fans in the world. I'm second from the right, front row

he was talking about, and console myself with the reflection that, while I might not know pressed duck from roast goose, I could always get the best table in a crowded restaurant, just by mentioning my name.

A good friend of mine, as my career blossomed out with Rangers, was none other than Ferenc Puskas, the great Hungarian inside-forward. As mentioned earlier, I first met Ferenc when I played for the Rest of the World against England in the FA Centenary International, at Wembley in 1963. He was a man after my own heart. He couldn't speak English, but we still had two things very much in common. He liked a good dram. And he had a good left foot.

Also he was extremely fond of the ladies. His problem was, he kept finding himself last in that particular queue. Being usually first, I was always glad to give him a hand. After the London game, I gave him the appropriate introductions, and he made excellent use of them, but I remember best the aftermath of another game involving Puskas – Rangers versus Real Madrid in the European Cup, in Glasgow.

Real were still a wonderful side then, and they beat us 1–0. Puskas, inevitably, was the scorer. It wasn't the only score he made that night. At the hotel afterwards, he lost no time in seeking me out.

'Baxter, Baxter, party, party, whisky, jig-a-jig.' He may not have been able to speak English in the accepted sense, but he knew how to make himself understood in the basics.

'Hold on a minute, Push,' I said. 'I'll let you know what's happening, don't worry. Would I let you down?' Quite charitable of me, when I think of it, considering the way he had treated us on the park.

As soon as we could, we went up to the George Hotel, headquarters for me and most of my friends then. Ferenc and two other Real Madrid players came along – I couldn't have kept him away – and we learned there that Ronnie McKinnon knew of a party out at Drumchapel.

Now Drumchapel, reckoned to be the biggest council-housing estate in Europe, might not strike you immediately as the ideal party spot for players from two of the best-known football clubs in the world. The truth is that there were lots of great parties at Drumchapel, there being only one snag. Few of the council houses had more than two bedrooms, which can make matters quite awkward at times for those who like a certain amount of privacy.

To get a bedroom, you had to be there early, and we weren't early. But Puskas wanted his whisky and his jig-a-jig, not necessarily in that order, and not necessarily separately. It was an attitude for which I had great respect and, as I had said, I couldn't let him down. Eventually, we paired him off with a very inventive lady who worked for a nationally known food firm. She seemed to like Ferenc, and neither was concerned about exactly where or how they could get together!

That was Drumchapel. But I had nothing against London. After I went to Sunderland, trips to London were common enough, and I still retained many of my friends in Glasgow and Edinburgh. It was an Edinburgh friend who, after an FA Cup Final, booked two suites for three nights at the Royal Garden, and laid on all the trimmings, and I mean *all*. That was one of the wildest week-ends I ever had. I don't know what it cost him, but if he reads this, he should be told that it was money well spent.

Dave Mackay's favourite club was the Astor, and we were there so often it became a sort of home from home. I met Johnny Haynes there, and Johnny was then earning his much-publicized £100-a-week-plus with Fulham. I liked him a lot. Apart from being a really good footballer, his tastes coincided with mine.

Ian St. John introduced me to another Johnny – Johnny Speight the script-writer, a great character. He was at one party when Jimmy Tarbuck threatened to knock hell out of the actor Tom Bell. Apparently, Bell had been narking at Ian St. John – Bell couldn't hold the drink at all – and if Speight hadn't intervened, Tarbuck might have ruined Bell's profile.

It was Johnny Speight who took us to a pub in Fulham, a well-known haunt of actors and actresses – although there were times when it wasn't too easy to tell the difference. George Kinnell was there with me, and it was eight in the morning before that party finished. We were not in the best of nick, to look at. But in fine spirits.

This might have been more forgiveable had it been a Sunday morning. It was Thursday. We had had a game the previous evening, and another coming up on the Saturday. We barely made it back to the hotel in time to bolt some breakfast – all for show, we didn't want any – and catch the 9.30 train back to Sunderland.

At the station the manager, Ian McColl, warned everybody that drinking on the train would be punished by a heavy fine. The exception would be one bottle of beer at lunch-time. Kinnell and I looked at each other, and the words didn't have to be spoken. A beer at lunch-time. Yes, that'll be right. Certainly we were in no mood to listen to that kind of instruction, and, frankly, I don't think Ian McColl really expected us to listen. But he couldn't have known that we had been up all night and hadn't drawn a sober breath for at least ten hours.

Ten minutes up the line, and we made our way to the buffet. Twenty minutes up the line, and we were once again feeling no pain whatsoever. The process is, I believe, called topping-up. An attractive Norwegian lady joined us in the buffet, and she was soon singing away merrily. I recall the song: 'Seven drunken nights'. We taught her the lyrics, with variations. Well, we might have got away with it if George Kinnell hadn't gone right over the score. He's my cousin, and I have a lot of affection for him, but you just couldn't take him anywhere. That's what he says about me, too, so we're even.

George had a party-piece, an imitation of a comic

called 'Parrot Face' Davis. He would take out his teeth, borrow a hat, and I swear he didn't look unlike a parrot. Maybe he should have gone on the stage. I was beginning to wonder seriously if I might be able to teach the Norwegian lass something else, when he left the buffet. A couple of minutes later he was back, no teeth, and wearing an obviously expensive Homburg hat. There seemed only one thing to do. I grabbed the hat, and threw it out of the window.

It was all George's fault. He went a wee bit pale, as if he were suddenly becoming all sober again. 'Jim,' he said, 'you know whose hat that is?' A silly question, you must admit. How could I have guessed it was the chairman's hat?

Nobody was pleased. Ian McColl could see now that we had not obeyed his orders to the letter. What made everything worse was the fact that some member of the public had spotted earlier on that George and I were having a right old party, and had somehow managed to tip off the Press. But that's a trick that can work both ways, and at another station, possibly York, McColl was told that reporters were waiting for us at Sunderland. Durham was not a scheduled stop for that train, but that's where it did stop, for just long enough to deposit us two on the platform.

'What'll we do now?' asked George, as we stood there, carrying our overnight bags.

'No problem,' I said. 'The nearest pub.'

Well, Durham isn't so very far from Sunderland. From the pub I made a couple of phone calls, and we got a lift home, easily enough. I forget what the score was on the Saturday, but on the Monday we were called into the manager's room and given a serious dressing-down. This didn't worry us as much as the financial punishment – a £300 fine for me, and £200 for George. This didn't strike me as quite fair, but I didn't see any point in making an official complaint.

That fine, incidentally, was paid. Every penny of it, so much a week. It was very painful.

Another London experience will be remembered by John Greig as readily as by myself. It was after the 1967 Wembley game, and, although we had made monkeys out of England, big Jackie Charlton invited some of us to a backstage theatre party. Not a bad lad, big Jack, considering that he was not only English but a Leeds United player. We went there from the Café Royal, and found still more heavily-laden buffet tables, with the usual champagne and brandy, etc., on the side.

It was young Jim McCalliog's first international, and he was wide-eyed at all the show-business nonsense going on. Darling this, and darling that, and a good scattering of big names like Jimmy Edwards, Frankie Howerd and Cilla Black. Luckily, there were also dozens of chorus girls there, too, and we all had a rare old time. Except for big John Greig.

In 1967 John wasn't too well versed in the ways of the world, and three of us – Denis Law, Billy Bremner and myself – decided to wind him up.

'Here, John,' I said, 'watch that Frankie Howerd. See the way he's eyeing you up.' Denis and Billy weighed in similarly, whenever they passed John – 'Has he made a move, yet, big man?' – and I suspect John was starting to get really worried, when there was a welcome distraction. Welcome for him, anyway.

Cilla Black, whom I never rated much as a singer, started to patronize us, in that Scouse accent of hers. It was the 'Jock' and 'haggis' bit, and she even had the nerve to suggest that Scotland had been lucky to win at Wembley.

That was too much for Billy Bremner. First, he compared her very unfavourably with Dusty Springfield. Then he expressed astonishment that Cilla, with such a face, had ever managed to get into show-biz at all. She was also, according to Billy, so thick that she couldn't get her own name right without an auto-cue. It might not have been the ideal behaviour for a guest at a party, but high-and-mighty Miss Black deserved it. We left very soon after that, which was probably just as well.

*

There must be hundreds of players who don't take a drink, but in my football career I've known only three – Davy Wilson, Ian McMillan and Alfredo di Stefano. As for players who didn't like the ladies, well, I'm glad to say I never met any. If I did, I don't think I would mention them by name, in case of defamation of character.

Both of these diversions are well catered for, perhaps surprisingly, in the Iron Curtain countries. Oh, I know they like to put on a prim and proper face, looking down with distaste at the decadence and the immorality of the West, but if you get the right people to show you the right places, they can be very lively. Budapest, for example, has lots of good night-clubs, and, unlike London, they don't want an arm and a leg for a couple of drinks. Warsaw is some place, too, but I may be prejudiced since I've always admired the Poles, as footballers and as people.

The only real problem I can remember was in Bratislava. It's in Czechoslovakia, near the Austrian border, and the Czechs like to play international matches there. It's smaller and less sophisticated than Prague, which isn't easy. The idea is probably to sicken the opposition by the claustrophobic atmosphere of both the city and the stadium. They sickened Scotland, all right, during the qualifying rounds of the 1962 World Cup, winning 4–0.

We were feeling depressed by the four-goal defeat, and badly needed to be cheered up. It is traditional, after a game abroad, for the players to be let off the leash for a few hours and, on this occasion, the SFA respected that tradition – although, in view of the result, one or two of the hierarchy must have regretted the decision.

After the lagers and the Bacardis – staple alcoholic beverages of footballers – our thoughts turned to other matters. We had been well warned not to cause any trouble, the local police being known to distrust foreigners, especially foreigners with too much drink inside them. And Bratislava had no great reputation for night clubs.

Enter Stan the student. We had met him earlier on the

trip, and we called him Stan because it was the only way we could pronounce his first name. We had given him tickets for the game, and had even taken a clothes collection for him, any shirts, slacks, etc. which we could spare. Given the austerity of Czechoslovakia – a ball-point pen was worth a fortune – Stan may have started a boutique, for all I know. He had said he would see us after the game, to show us around the town. We weren't at all sure he would turn up, but he did, all smiles and broken English, which was at least better than our command of his own language.

I took him aside, in the foyer of our hotel. 'Look,' I said, 'never mind showing us the town. How about bringing some birds over?' He didn't understand fully at first, but sign-language helped. Hoping for the best, we repaired to the bar to await Stan's return. Somebody, I won't say who, said he hoped Stan had a charabanc, because he'd need it. No more than half-an-hour passed, and Stan was back with a couple of darlings. I cheered up almost immediately. There was no charabanc, but I was always optimistic. Other faces fell.

'Yes,' said Stan, 'I know, but it is late. I can do no better, and they are nice girls, are they not?.'

I assured him that there was no problem so far as that was concerned and, to be truthful, I thought he hadn't done too badly.

'There is something else,' said Stan. 'It does not look too good.'

What was he on about now? Were the girls going to have a quick drink and take off? Was he kidding us along? It transpired, however, that a couple of the hotel porters had seen Stan and the girls come in. They were watching carefully to make sure they didn't go upstairs.

'Give them a few bob,' I suggested, following up with a gesture towards the porters' desk and rubbing the thumb and forefinger together in the international sign for hard cash.

Stan looked sad. These porters were bad news, it seemed. He didn't say outright that they worked for the

Czech version of the KGB in their spare time, but one got the message.

Resourceful as ever, and wits sharpened by the glances I was getting from the tall one, I turned to Denis Law and Paddy Crerand.

'Denis,' I said, 'Paddy. There's only one thing to do. You two start a fight, and make it look good. That'll attract the attention of these buggers, and we'll get the lassies up the stairs.'

To their credit, that's what Denis and Paddy did, with Pat Quinn, Ian Ure and Davie Herd cheering them on. Meanwhile, guess who was rushing up the stairs with a pretty lady on each arm? I appreciate that that sounds a little selfish, but there wasn't a lot of choice, and all's fair in love and war, as they say.

You may now be under the impression that I'm boasting. Well, no, I didn't accommodate both girls. I may be selfish at times, but I'm not greedy. I was given a bit of help, but, in the cause of domestic peace in a certain household, I'm not saying from whom.

Then there was Vienna. Was there ever a city with such good and bad memories for anybody? In Vienna I played one of the best games of my life, got a broken leg in the last minute – and then found wonderful consolation. The first hour or so after the leg-break is somewhat hazy, with ambulance sirens screaming, men in white coats fussing about, and plenty of pain.

I do remember, however, with some clarity, a terrible feeling of disappointment. Not so much because of the injury – I had accepted that as one more occupational hazard – but because two of my friends from Scotland had promised to come up to my hotel room later on, and to bring suitable entertainment. For a bad moment, it even crossed my mind that I might have to stay in hospital overnight. But I was taken back to the hotel, the crippled hero of the hour, and was beginning to feel a little better.

Scot Symon, that marvellous gentleman, wanted to

stay with me, while the others went to the banquet. You could see he was truly worried, father-like, about me. Also, I suppose he thought I'd be lonely and fed up. It was a nice thought but, much though I respected Scot, I didn't really see him in the role of cheer-leader.

'Don't worry, boss,' I said. 'I'll be fine, honest. Anyway, a couple of friends should be up to see me. We'll have a game of cards, and a bottle of beer.'

Scot looked doubtful. Maybe I shouldn't have mentioned the beer. But he agreed to go to the banquet. 'Try to get a good rest,' he said.

He couldn't have been as far as the lift before I was on to room service, ordering brandy, champagne, Black Label, soft drinks, a bucket of ice, and three fillet-steak suppers. At least, I told myself, I could have a wee bevy.

My two friends arrived a few minutes later, presumably having seen Scot leave. So did the room-service waiter. We were busy making serious inroads into the food and drink, getting quite merry, swapping lies, when one of them picked up the telephone.

'Ah, well,' he said, 'if the mountain won't come to Muhammed, then Muhammed will just have to go to the mountain.' He's drunk already, I thought. And he's only had about half a bottle. 'Don't worry,' he said, 'I've got a wee surprise for you.'

I still didn't know what he was talking about until, maybe an hour later, the wee surprise knocked at the door. She was a beauty, and she was full of sympathy for 'Jeem', who, it now transpired, had beaten Rapid Vienna all on his own. She wasn't a nurse, either. Not, at any rate, a nurse in the normal sense of the word. I can only say I never had a better one. The plaster was still steaming, and so was I, but it's amazing what can be done in such circumstances, and if there's plenty of time. My 'nurse' stayed until morning, and I confess I didn't follow too closely Scot's instruction to get a good rest. It was a good night, though.

It was so good, in fact, that I saw no reason why there

shouldn't be an encore the next night. That was where Rangers became something of a nuisance.

All the newspapers told the story of how Vienna Airport was closed by fog, of how I was taken part of the way to Salzburg by ambulance, and of how I stopped that ambulance after 40 miles – saying that my leg just couldn't take the bumping about. The truth is that I had telephoned the wee surprise, and she had agreed to be back in order to continue the nursing treatment.

The ploy, of course, went wrong. Scot Symon, still thinking of my welfare, also came back to Vienna – and arranged special accommodation on a train to Salzburg. I couldn't see any way out of that. You can hardly start moaning about the train being too bumpy.

Meanwhile, every time I see my mate, I call him Muhammed, and it costs me a double.

Sweden is famous for the quality and the friendliness of its women. This fame is well justified.

When Rangers played the East German team Vorwaerts in the European Cup, there was some diplomatic difficulty, and the away leg was played in Malmo, Sweden. This suited us very well. I have said some quite complimentary things about how the Eastern bloc countries can be enjoyable, but East Germany is a glaring exception.

The match was scheduled for the Tuesday evening and, just after lunch, we went through the ritual of collecting spending-money from the club, such money being intended to buy presents for family and friends back home.

Into a department store we strolled, three of us – big Bill Paterson, Billy Stevenson and myself. Bill Paterson was a really macho, handsome type, definitely in the top league when it came to the ladies. He was so good at chatting up that I would often just let him get on with it, so long as I was reasonably sure that I'd get my share of whatever was going.

He didn't waste any time with a couple of the assistants. It occurred to me that Billy Stevenson was out in the cold, but that was his problem. There were plenty more, especially in Sweden. We gave the girls – tall, blonde, just what you'd expect – match tickets, and arranged to see them later. We left the store, thinking that the shopping was making satisfactory progress. Our next meeting with these two girls came sooner than was planned, and I doubt if Scot Symon will ever forget it. It took place, believe it or not, in the Rangers dressing-room.

Now at Ibrox, in Scotland come to that, nobody who isn't supposed to be there, gets into the dressing-room before a game. In Sweden, nobody bothers about such rules and restrictions. I was tying my boot-laces, and some players were in various stages of undress, when the two Swedish girls knocked. I can't remember who actually opened the door, but whoever it was didn't have the nerve to keep them out.

They carried bouquets of flowers. One spotted Bill, ran up to him, planted a big kiss on his mouth, and gave him a bouquet. The other said: 'Where's my one?' I'm glad to say she didn't mean Billy Stevenson. 'Ah, Jim, Jim,' she trilled, and for me, too, there were flowers and a kiss. What was Scot Symon, manager of the Rangers Football Club doing, all this time? Absolutely nothing. He must have been in a state of shock. I wouldn't be surprised if he still is. As it turned out, the evening match was called off after about 20 minutes because of fog, and the continuation of hostilities was scheduled for half-past-nine the next morning.

You couldn't blame Scot Symon for laying down a strict eleven p.m. curfew when we arrived back at the hotel. No drinkies, no ladies. Just a long, health-giving sleep. After all, it was the European Cup.

In the hotel restaurant we quickly spotted two lovely looking ladies at a corner table. They looked over, smiled and waved. I thought, oh, ho, this looks very, very promising. But how about the curfew? What curfew, I thought again, hoping that Scot Symon hadn't seen the girls wave.

Bill Paterson was at another table, looking quite anxious. 'What's the strength here, then, Bill?' I said. 'Are you on?' But I realized why he was looking anxious. He didn't want to know. To Bill, James Scotland Symon was a man who had to be obeyed. To him, a curfew was a curfew, and eleven o'clock didn't mean five-past-eleven.

What a waste! All that expert chatting-up, and for what? But it put me in a spot. I suppose I could have managed both, but, as we have noted, it *was* a European Cup tie, and there are limits. Moreover, the other one might not have fancied me. Well, you can never be sure.

But another team-mate – let's just call him Cyril – was more than willing to find out a bit more about Swedish gymnastics and, as soon as it was safe, I gave the girls the room key. 'We'll be up shortly,' I told them. 'Have yourselves a drink, there's plenty.' As indeed there was, all duty free.

First, I had to impress upon Willie Henderson, who was rooming with me – it was one of his first trips – that I didn't want any nonsense from him. He could have Cyril's bed, and I told him the number.

It must have been about half-past-eleven when the phone rang in my room. At that moment, Cyril and I were enjoying ourselves immensely and so too, I hope, were the girls. Not best pleased, I decided I had better answer the bloody thing. It was Jimmy Millar, panic-stricken.

'Stanley,' he hissed, 'you'd better get those girls out of there, and fast. Davie Kinnear's on the warpath. He's flaming.'

I couldn't understand it. How did Kinnear, the trainer, know? He didn't usually go around hotel bedrooms, checking like a guard at a concentration camp. It was only later we discovered how. He had found wee Willie Henderson wandering round the hotel corridors like a lost sheep, having forgotten Cyril's room number.

'Who're you rooming with?' asked Kinnear.

'Baxter', said wee Willie, who couldn't think of anything else to say, having also forgotten who Cyril was rooming with.

'Baxter!' shouted Kinnear, who was not one of my closest friends. 'By the holy . . .'

We got the girls out of the room just in time. We pushed them into a room occupied by Davie Provan and Bobby King, thinking that it's no loss what a friend gets. When Davie Kinnear hammered at our door, we were lying on the beds, chatting. He knew Cyril was in the wrong room.

'What are you two doing?'

We looked at him innocently. 'Talking tactics,' we said. 'What else?'

There are folk who say that Rod Stewart merely pretends to have an interest in football, especially Scottish football, for the sake of publicity. They should know better. Or they should beware the sin of envy.

Rod is probably a millionaire several times over, but let me assure you that his enthusiasm for the game is real. I'd go so far as to say that he is fanatical. He is only just that wee bit more fanatical about his profession!

A few years ago, I played with Rod. It was the first time I ever met him, and he was a guest for an ex-Scotland XI against an ex-England XI at Dam Park, Ayr. It was all for charity, of course, and Rod's presence was extremely important. How did he play? Well, I must be quite honest. He was keen, very keen, which covers a multitude of sins. I'm not saying he couldn't play. I'm saying he tried very hard, and, believe me, I've seen a lot worse.

If he should ever read this, I hope he won't take offence. My second meeting with Rod followed a call from one of his mates, a lad who usually accompanied him on tour. Scotland were due to play a World Cup qualifying game, and the message from Rod was . . . 'see you in your pub at half-past-six, for a couple of drinks.'

At half-past-six, he hadn't arrived. A couple of the regulars wondered if it was a bit of flannel. Then, 15 minutes later, came a call from Renfrew Airport control. The plane had been delayed, and would we please hold the tickets? That, I remember thinking at the time, was style.

Rod duly arrived, in good time for the eight o'clock kick-off, and that night we talked about football... yes, all night. The choice of conversation wasn't mine, I stress. I wanted to know about Britt Ekland. He preferred to talk about Kenny Dalglish and Denis Law.

To emphasize that he is a genuine fan, there's another similar story. I was at the opening of a disco with him, a place called 'Panama Jax'. We went back to his hotel later on, the Holiday Inn in Glasgow, and we talked about football until the dawn was breaking. Mind you, there was plenty of champagne to oil the old vocal chords.

But can you imagine it? Stewart and Baxter in a fancy hotel from midnight to almost breakfast-time – and not a bird in sight! Listen, I'll take an oath on it. I only hope that story hasn't ruined our reputations.

Another of my favourite pop-singers is Little Richard. When I was on tour with Sunderland in Vancouver, he was giving a concert at 'La Cave' night-club, and all of the players were there. After the concert, we thought it would be a good idea to give him a call, and it so happened that I was quite friendly with the receptionist at his hotel. She revealed the suite number, and up we went... myself, George Kinnell and a couple of the younger players.

We had all had a fair refreshment, and we had a few more in the suite, but only for about ten minutes. The dope was being passed around, and the place started to resemble a Baghdad brothel.

As may have been noticed by perceptive readers, I am quite broadminded, but there are limits. Dope is not my game, and I don't have much interest in those who disagree.

I still love Little Richard's recordings, but I'm delighted to see that he is a Gospel singer now, a born-again Christian. He has seen the light, you might say. Good for him, too!

14

North American interludes

Again we had won the treble. We were doing well. At that time, 1963, Celtic didn't matter, and I don't know where Jock Stein was. Rangers were top boys, and everybody and his auntie wanted us. That's what happens, when a Scottish side like Rangers or Celtic does really well. Expatriate Scots in Canada, Australia, New Zealand, you name it, they want to see the lads play. Frankly, they would probably want to see Scottish sides play regardless of domestic success.

I really love these fans. They are their own people, but they never forget their roots. It's not just nostalgia, it's not just sentiment. It's pride. They *are* Canadians, they *are* Australians, they *are* New Zealanders. But there's always this great feeling for Scotland. You never want to let them down. You always try hard for them on the tours, the so-called junkets, because you know they are expecting a good show, and you know they deserve a good show.

Certainly a Scottish side goes to those countries for a high old time. The hospitality, for a start, is staggering. But even if you get up at eight in the morning, with an appalling well-earned hang-over, not having gone to bed before six, you *do* get up. That's the point. We could always play football so much better than the local sides that it wasn't a contest. It isn't a question of winning, even. It's about playing real football.

And that, I like to think, is the reason why, along with Willie Henderson, I was invited in 1963 to play three summer games in Canada – at £200 a game, with all expenses. In present-day terms, that has to be multiplied oh, ten times say?

But we were not told about it by the club. Please don't ask me why. I would have to give the old answer, quoting chairman John Lawrence, who had so much money he couldn't have spent it in a hundred years – unless, of course, he were to do a Hugh Fraser and try roulette. We knew about the Canadian offer through the Press, and this pushed Rangers into an official statement. It was made by Scot Symon:

'The Rangers board has decided that Baxter and Henderson, after a very hard season, need a rest. This is in the interests of the Rangers Football Club but, at least as importantly, in their own interest.'

When I read that, I was looking for walls to climb up. Think about it! Here's me, 23 years old, playing like I might never play again, on top of the world, seeking enjoyment everywhere – and they wouldn't let me go to Canada. True, I didn't know anything about Canada then. As if I cared. It was something different, it wouldn't be like playing the Czechs or the Brazilians, and the money was magic.

'Boss,' I said to Scot Symon, 'do me a favour. When I signed for Rangers, what did you tell me? You told me that Rangers would open doors for me all over the world, that's what you told me. Now here we have a door opening, and you're slamming it right in my face. It's not as if we'll be knocking our brains out. It's a holiday with football. All we have to do is play a few games, and we're getting £200 a time. Come on, boss, come on.'

He held firm. 'You might get hurt,' he said.

'What, get hurt? When do I get hurt? Turn it up, boss. We're not going to be playing the Celtic. We won't even be playing Partick Thistle. I'm telling you again, it's a holiday, with a bit of football thrown in.'

Still he held firm. 'Sorry, Jim. I'm giving you the decision of the board. You are not, repeat not, going to Canada. What's wrong with you, aren't you getting paid enough here?.' That was an argument I did not pursue at that particular time. I was too angry.

The above conversation took place shortly before the start of the banquet at the St. Enoch Hotel, a banquet meant to celebrate the winning of the treble. We were, in fact, in the hotel, with wives and sweethearts hovering around.

'Fair enough, boss,' I said, 'but I'll tell you one thing, I'm not going to your banquet.'

Scot looked at me sourly. 'Oh, yes, Jim, you're going to the banquet, whether you like it or not.'

It was a stand-off. I got up, and walked through to the bar.

'What's the matter with you?' asked Helen, the barmaid. A fine lass was Helen, but she couldn't cheer me up that night. Nor could my pal, the banqueting manager.

'What's the matter with me?' I said. 'Give us a large Bacardi. Give us three large Bacardis. I'm choked. I've been offered three games in Canada at £200 a time, plus maybe a bit of coaching, not a penny piece out of my own pocket, and Rangers have knocked me back. That's what's the matter with me.'

I'm not sure how many Bacardis I did have, before the word came. The banquet was about to start. Scot approached me, as if I were a piranha he had betted he would pat on the head. I honestly felt sympathy for him. It's just as well the chairman hadn't tried it.

'Jim,' said Scot, 'we're waiting for you.'

My mind was made up. They could wait all night. They could take their banquet, and they knew what they could do with it. I said to Scot: 'Boss, I don't want to fall out with you. Just don't ask me. I'm not going.'

He knew then that I meant what I said. He turned away and, bacardi or not, I felt another wave of sympathy for him. It wasn't his fault. Yet it wasn't my fault, either.

I walked down the stairs of the hotel, out into Argyle Street. It's often said that, when you have had a few drinks, the fresh air has a bad effect, makes you feel suddenly legless. Rubbish! I stalked along Argyle Street, under the Highlandman's Umbrella – that's the railway line from Central Station, in case you didn't know, or come from Edinburgh – about as far as York Street.

I had a large bacardi, as if I needed it, in, I think, the Waterloo Bar, ignoring any glances of recognition. It was not my night for fans, I'm sorry to say.

The hell with it! Back I went to the hotel. It must have been later than I imagined, because the banquet was finishing. Yet still they tried to get me in, as if I wanted cheese and biscuits. Bobby Shearer came out, so did one of the directors, John F. Wilson.

'Come on, Jim. Come in and have a brandy.'

'Piss off,' I said. 'Nothing personal. Bollocks to the banquet.'

I stayed in the bar, as the banqueting room emptied, as everybody except the staff went home. And the staff was cleaning up, hoovering away like mad.

'Right,' I said, 'drinks for everybody. Anything you want.' The drinks came up, and I wasn't counting. I signed the bill.

Two weeks later I was in Edmonton, Canada. Obviously I can't be sure what the Rangers directors said to each other after that banquet. Just as obviously, they decided that, after all, they could spare me. I had made my point, and I had won. Wee Willie Henderson, I'm sorry to say, stayed at home.

So it wasn't easy to get to Canada. But the battle proved well worth while, perhaps not immediately, but in the fullness of time. In that summer of 1963, I played in the scheduled games, never breaking sweat, and, just like royalty, started other games merely by kicking off. I was what one might call a celebrity.

The seeds of goodwill were sown. That year, a great wee lad called Alex Johnstone – he's probably still there – used to drive me around, and one day he took me down to Edmonton Customs. I had to pick up a box of

Rangers souvenirs – badges, pennants, that kind of thing – which Scot Symon had, very kindly, sent out. As I keep on saying, Scot was a gentleman. He never did bear a grudge.

There was another Scots lad on the Customs, but I admit I couldn't look at anybody but Sue. Sue was half-caste, and an absolute stunner. She has always reminded me of Dorothy Dandridge, the star of the film, *Carmen Jones*.

The Scottish Customs man gave me an introduction. I told her I was going to a function that night on my own, and that I didn't like being on my own. Would she come along? The function was a football match, and I had Sue on my arm in the directors' box. I left her for about two minutes, while I nipped down to kick off, thumping the ball high in the air, to show how pleased I was. The directors, like all Canadians, were very understanding.

When I left Canada that summer, I never thought I'd see Sue again, a prospect which didn't please me at all. She really was a beautiful woman. Funny how life works out, to coin a phrase.

Three years later, I was playing for Sunderland, and what do you think? Sunderland arranged a trip to Canada and the USA. First stop – Vancouver.

Now Vancouver is a fair old distance from Edmonton, and when we arrived there, Sue was very much on my mind. The very word 'Canada' conjured up pleasant visions of her, but optimism could be taken too far.

A telegram was waiting for me at the Vancouver hotel. It gave a telephone number. 'Please call. Sue.' It's a few years ago, but I'm pretty sure I telephoned before I went up to my room. Sue was not only still in Canada, she was right there in Vancouver – and she was the mayor's secretary. This was like winning the treble chance in an eight-draw week.

'You know we're going to the mayor's reception tomorrow night?' I said.

'Oh yes,' she said. 'And I'll be there.'

As I strolled into that reception the following night, I

had about five hundred Canadian dollars in my pocket, and I had told only one person – my cousin, George Kinnell – about sweet Sue.

The other Sunderland players saw Sue before I did. Or they thought they did. There was nobody else remotely in her class, and they were positively drooling.

'Calm down, calm down,' I said to them. 'It's only another bird, isn't it? Let's face it, there's a lot of it about. You'd think you were wee boys. Watch your pimples.' They knew that I wasn't exactly a Boy Scout myself, and they knew, furthermore, that I was very partial to the opposite sex. And that I had an excellent track-record in that respect. But this was going too far, they said, even for me.

'Tell you what,' I said. 'I've got a few dollars on me. See that bird? She'll be with me at the dinner table tonight. Who fancies a bet?'

Some of the lads looked at me strangely, but every cent of the five hundred dollars was covered, at even money. Maybe they suspected something, and the terms of the bet were precisely worked out, as if I were trying to trick them or something. True, I did have some form to go on, but it was all above board, as far as I was concerned.

George Kinnell and I had a few drinks in my room with Sue, all pre-arranged, before entering the dining-room at nine p.m., the appointed hour, the bet duly won.

If only I could have made yet another arrangement – for a photographer to record for posterity the faces of my Sunderland team-mates.

Never mind your Paul Newman, never mind your Robert Redford. This was James Baxter, just a simple old footballing man, and if you believe that, you'll believe anything. It wasn't fair, to be sure it wasn't fair. But when you get the chance of a hundred per cent, no-money-back, waterproof, ironclad certainty, at even money, what would you do? Ask for a stewards' inquiry?

If Charlie Hurley or George Mulhall or Neil Martin or John Park ever reads this, and if they are not happy about the money they lost, I can tell them exactly what they can do. They can sue me.

That was a good tour of the United States with Sunderland. In 1966 soccer was just starting to catch on over there, but it was in the capital of the good old USA that I got one of the biggest frights of my life. Washington DC, no less, and we were staying at the Hilton Hotel. We should never have left that area, which was reasonably safe, but Aberdeen were also touring at the time, and Jim Storey – who also played for Airdrie and Leeds – said he had found this great club a few miles away.

What he didn't tell us was that the club was situated in a district with a population 70 per cent black. I have absolutely no racial prejudice, but that statistic mattered, as I will explain.

It was a good club, fair drink prices, lots of beautiful black girls who didn't mind dancing, and high-class jazz. Well, cross my heart, I don't remember offending anybody, but, at about two o'clock in the morning, John Park and I were the only footballers left in the place, and we were not sober.

Time to call it a night, we decided, and there we were out on the pavement, swaying slightly, seeking a taxi. I was slightly disappointed at the failure to pull any of the girls – and me in my favourite outfit, black slacks, black polo jersey, black-and-white houndstooth jacket – but you had to be philosophical about such things. At that moment, a big car skidded to a halt beside us, and three large black fellows started to get out. They looked very handy. 'There's the bastards,' one of them shouted.

I glanced around nervously. The street was deserted. 'Parky,' I said, 'they've got to be talking to us. What d'you think?' John Park, and I swear this is true, said: 'Let's have a go at them!'

'That'll be right,' I said, and got off my mark. It's not easy to run at all after 15 bacardis, American measures, even if fear *is* supposed to lend wings to your heels. Next thing I know, one of the lads is on my back, I'm on the pavement, and he's using me as a punch-bag. Suddenly he stopped punching, and I was wondering whether his knuckles were sore or whether he was trying to find a knife with which to remove parts of the Baxter anatomy. Then I heard the siren, too.

It was like a James Cagney film. The bloke went off down the street, Olympic style, and the squad-car stopped beside where I was sitting, bruised and bloodied. At home, I wouldn't have needed to say who I was. They would have known. As far as these Washington cops were concerned, I was just one more street brawler.

'Get your hands up, buddy!'

'Hang on a minute, lads, it was all . . .'

One of them then gave me a couple of right-handers, as if I hadn't had enough already, and I was thrown into the back of the car. Who was sitting there, all in one piece, but John Park? He could always run faster than me.

Down at the precinct, the sergeant stared cynically, as we explained who we were. I don't think he really knew what soccer was. 'Look, don't take our word for it,' I pleaded, 'phone the Hilton and ask for Mr McColl.' We were slung into the cells while he made up his mind. Eventually he did phone the Hilton and, as he let us go, he told us how lucky we had been to escape alive from that particular district.

And, of course, poor Ian McColl's sleep was ruined again. He must have understood what Don Revie meant when he said he would like to sign J.B., but that he preferred to sleep at nights.

The more I think about Ian McColl, the more affection I have for the man. As I have related, he lost much sleep over those who were in his charge, notably people like me and George Kinnell, who was always aspiring to the First Division of booze and bets. A division of which, let me say without boasting, I was undisputed champion. But not even Ian could have suspected, or predicted in his more pessimistic moments, what happened a couple of days after we had landed in Vancouver. To be precise, it happened one day after our arrival at the Georgian Towers, which was our hotel headquarters for that seven-week stay on the great continent of North America.

Now let me state right away that Ian had made it very plain to us that we were on holiday... with a bit of work, like occasionally playing football, thrown in to pay some of the expenses.

He would say: 'Look, I know you're all going to get well full, night after night, and I do not even want to guess what you'll be doing in your horrible little bedrooms. But when you have to play football, I want you to play football. We do not sell people short. All right?'

In fact, it *was* all right. We cut a swathe through the pubs, clubs and hotels of North America, like a combine harvester. We still played football. We represented various temporary clubs... Sunderland, for example, were the Royal Canadians. Aberdeen were Washington Diplomats. Dundee United were there, too, and so were Hibs.

Should I take a certain pride, or conceit, in the fact that a Toronto newspaper made a comparison between Kinnell and me on the one hand, and Joe Namath on the other? Joe Namath? Come on, now, you know who he was. The greatest quarter-back in the history of American football and one of the finest, most dedicated party-goers in the history of America, never mind mere football.

Joe was a millionaire, which was more than I was. He built an enormous reputation in the hell-raising stakes. The Toronto newspaper said that, compared with Kinnell and Baxter, he was a mere choirboy. I have never found out how Joe, a man obviously after my own heart, replied to that insult. Or even *if* he did. I don't suppose I ever will.

But to get back to our first morning in Vancouver. The

journey had been fairly uneventful, despite the duty-free and other aspects of airline hospitality – if that's the word for something which costs far too much anyway. The stewardesses were, as ever, smiling brightly, sometimes meaning it, sometimes not, but I have always distrusted airline stewardesses. If you try to take any liberties, they have this anti-social habit of pouring hot coffee over your best trousers at the first available opportunity.

And so we checked in. We slept well, as we were entitled to, having crossed the Atlantic and America on blissful waves of the very best 70% proof. We did not wake up so well. Vancouver shower-compartments are highly efficient, but I never did fancy the cold-water bit, which is said to be high in recuperative qualities, and it must have been around half-past-ten in the morning when I scraped the goo from my eyes, shoved down a pint of orange juice – real juice from squeezed oranges – and said to Kinnell:

'What are we going to do now, then?'

I think it is to the credit of us both that there was no suggestion which related, even remotely, to breakfast. All over the hotel, so far as I knew, they were tucking into bacon, eggs, sausages, waffles, you name it. George, that excellent room-mate, said:

'How about ordering a few halves?'

For the benefit of those who don't know any better, a half is not a half-pint of your best bitter. It is a measure of whisky, gin, vodka, brandy, rum, Barcardi or whatever. That's in the west of Scotland. In the east, it's a nip. After all these years with Rangers, though, I had become well westernized. In Vancouver, I became rather more so.

'A few halves?' I said to George. 'What a good idea, son!'

If there's one thing absolutely undeniable about North American hotels – especially in Vancouver, and more especially the Georgian Towers – it's the standard of service. Five stars are said to be the best. The Georgian was a galaxy. In no time at all, we had a crate of bacardi, a crate of Black Label, a crate of French champagne, plus lots and lots of the appropriate mixers. We even had Guinness and, as is known to one and all, there is no drink in all the world like champagne and Guinness when one is trying to feel better.

The consignment was brought up from the local drug-store, or off-licence, or anything else they liked to call it. It was then consigned to the cave-like refrigerator which stood, in a corner of the room, like one of the pyramids. A big ice-box, by any standards. We paid cash. George looked at this most admirable of gantries, and asked the 64-dollar question.

'Is this going to last us for seven weeks?'

I saw his point. We would be travelling around quite a lot, maybe 30,000 miles, give or take a few, but seven weeks? 'No,' I said.

We accepted the situation as it was, however, and then had several large ones. It wasn't even noon when the knock came at the door. A bad-tempered knock, a policeman's knock. I do not, by the way, pretend to be an expert in the way policemen knock at doors. I have been around a bit, but there are limits. Yet the knock remains recognizable. It goes 'boom boom' and then, almost immediately, in case you haven't got the message, 'boom boom' again.

The blood chills almost instinctively. If you have ever done anything wrong, if you have ever so much as neglected to pay a parking ticket, you frown anxiously. If you have done nothing wrong, you still frown anxiously.

We let them in. There were two of them. Sergeant Ken and his mate, Andy, presumably a rookie. They were plain-clothes boys, but they could have been picked out as coppers at the Rangers end of Hampden on a Scotland–England day. Suspicion leaped from their eyes, and their entire attitude made it plain that, if we hadn't opened the door, they would have broken it down and been delighted at the opportunity.

No time was wasted in preliminaries. They didn't take out Police Specials from shoulder-holsters. They had no reason to do so. We knew they meant it, and they knew that we knew. They went straight to the ice-box. For a joyful moment, it crossed my mind that all they wanted was a drink. The moment passed.

'This lot yours?' Ken asked.

We had receipts. We had paid, and we had paid in green Canadian dollars. Emboldened by this knowledge, I said: 'It's ours.' Trying hard, all the while, to look like Humphrey Bogart sneering at Chicago fuzz to whom he had paid plenty in hush-money and about whom he was shortly going to complain bitterly to the bosses.

'Where d'you get the money?'

This seemed an unreasonable question. Who did Sergeant Ken think we were? 'We earned it.'

'Is that right? Does it look anything like this, maybe?' Whereupon Sergeant Ken fished out 20 ten-dollar bills from his breast-pocket.

To me, a ten-dollar bill is a ten-dollar bill. 'Could be,' I said, though not feeling at all like Mr Bogart by this time.

'Forgeries,' he said. 'Counterfeit,' he said, ramming the point home. 'And every damned one traced right here, right to this hotel, right to this room.'

George spoke for the first time, and I wish he had kept his face shut. Imagine saying something like: 'There must be some mistake.' Talk about a line from a bad play!

Those pillars of the Vancouver Police Department, Ken and Andy, could hardly believe their luck. 'You bet there must be some mistake,' said Ken. 'Your mistake. Get your coats on.' His next line was as bad as George's. 'We'll talk about this down at the station.'

There was just one thing I could do. It wasn't so much begging for mercy, as pleading a wee bit. We were professional footballers, I told them. We were in Canada on a goodwill tour, and if they didn't believe us, for God's sake, they could call Ian McColl.

'Ian who?'

'He's our boss, the manager, a very respectable gent indeed, and he's in room 222.'

They agreed, with obvious reluctance. Perhaps they couldn't understand our Scottish accent, and they just gave us the benefit of the doubt.

When Ian arrived, looking his usual spruce self but with a worried expression for all that, he stared wildly at the two cops, then at us. Then his eyes moved to the fridge door, which had been left open as if intended to show its contents off.

'I don't believe this,' he wailed, and how could you blame him? 'You've only been here five minutes, and you've got half the Vancouver police force on your necks.' He could perhaps have been forgiven the exaggeration.

Ken came quickly to the point: 'These two', he said heavily, 'just bought all that booze.'

'Is that what it's all about?' said Ian quickly, and you could see his eyes light up with hope. 'Well, I know they shouldn't have, but they're probably going to share it around, and if they *did* pay for it, well, after all.'

'They paid for it,' said the sergeant, 'partly with counterfeit money. *This* counterfeit money!'

I was still bemused. Ian scratched his head. 'Where did you get that money?' he asked. 'Come on now, no fannying.'

Patiently, as the cops listened, we explained to him that the whole thing was obviously a terrible mistake. We cast no aspersions on the efficiency of the Vancouver police department, but surely, just this once, they had got their lines crossed on the way to our room. 'We may be a bit daft at times, boss,' I said, 'but forgery isn't our game. All the dollars we had, they came from the bank at Heathrow, and that's straight up.'

I meant it too. I knew very well that if there's one thing certain to get any police force in a turmoil, it's the passing of bad money. It attacks the foundation of society, or so they seem to think. By this time, Ken and Andy weren't quite so adamant. The suspicion was crossing their minds that a mistake could indeed have been made somewhere. Sensing a reprieve, Ian talked faster than ever, offering to pay the 200 dollars all over again, this time with the right stuff. 'Who's lost?' he asked. 'Only us.'

His argument prevailed. The climate changed quite suddenly. The cops sat down for a few drinks, and in no time at all we were actually friendly. The upshot was quite remarkable. We became so friendly, not only with Ken and Andy, but also with various of their colleagues, that we were using police cars as taxis for the rest of the seven-week trip. The lads would pick us up regularly, after parties, and make sure we got home safely. And they helped, on occasions, to get rid of all that booze. Which did have to be replenished.

Ken said later: 'When I opened the door of that icebox, and saw what was in it, I knew we had a right pair here.'

15

Easy come, easier go

Somebody once asked me how much I had lost, in my whole life, through gambling. I tried to answer, and my estimate was £50,000. Every time I remember that question and that answer, I remind myself of my own stupidity. For it's a lot more than that.

When I was a ten-year-old boy, back in Fife, I was always gambling. In Fife, and in most mining communities, gambling was a way of life. I have no doubt that, despite the way pits keep being closed down, it still is. Of course, there are lots of people in mining villages who never, ever bet. All I'm saying is that I never met any.

We could collect lemonade bottles to cash in for a couple of pennies, and we would have a 'tossing' school. The Australians, I think, call it 'two up'. The idea is to bet on whether two coins, tossed in the air, will come down both heads or both tails. It's not a sophisticated game, but it can be very expensive. For the actual coins become – when you get older – symbols. And hundreds of pounds can be won or lost on side-bets.

Then there was pontoon. The pontoon played in Fife and the Lothians – probably also in Ayrshire and Yorkshire, for all I know – should not be confused with the black-jack rubbish current in the casinos nowadays. This is no time to start comparing the different rules. Let me just say that if modern casino croupiers were to try to impose black-jack rules on a mining pontoon-school, they would have a chance to investigate, abruptly, the

134

depth of the nearest pit-shaft.

Of all the vices, if they can be called vices – after all, I enjoyed them greatly – there can surely be none quite so potentially disastrous as gambling. For me, the potential was fully realized.

You can spend a lot of money on drink, but you can only drink so much. You can spend a lot of money on women, but usually on only one at a time. But there is absolutely no limit to the damage that can be done, if you're a gambler. In a few seconds, literally, you can lose enough to take a lovely lass to Bermuda for a fortnight. By the same token, let's admit, you can win enough to take two lovely lassies to Bermuda for a month, but I'm sure you understand what I'm talking about.

When money becomes betting-vouchers, which can easily happen, you're in trouble, and you'd better not forget it. Even now, I'm not certain if I have beaten the gambling bug, the most vicious bug of the lot, but I think I just may have done it. If not, it won't be through lack of trying – or of hard and bitter experience.

At Ibrox, I thought I was underpaid – I *was* underpaid – but my cash in hand was still very much higher than the average wage. Week after week, I would blow the lot, mainly on the horses.

Naturally, you don't lose every day. You win enough, and regularly enough, to discourage the urge to cut your own throat. After four races, there's £400 down the drain, and on the fifth, there's £200 back. That lends confidence for the last race, and you go in, head down, and maybe win another £50. So you don't feel too bad. You have at least won *something*. That's what you tell yourself. And we're talking about one of the better days. Then suppose you have a real cracker of a day. A couple of grand up? That reinforces your faith in your own intelligence, and when you're three grand down by the end of the week, what do you remember? You remember the winners. You don't count what's in your pocket, what's in your bank balance. You're afraid to.

When I had my public house in Paisley Road West,

about a George Young free-kick from Ibrox, the money came in fast. It went out faster. There are not too many people without private oil-wells who can afford to bet in terms of thousands of pounds, and I was certainly not in that company. All the same, I tried hard enough. And so, perhaps on a Saturday, I'd begin with £100 bets, and, bolstered by Bacardi, progress to £200 or £300 bets. Before long, the takings had gone to Hills, Ladbrokes or Corals, and I'd be tapping – borrowing to the uninitiated – till the Monday.

I didn't mention Bacardi by accident, by the way. There is no more lethal combination, financially speaking, than betting and booze. When the drink is in, as the saying goes, the wit is out. Certainly it is possible to put £100 on a 10–1 winner, when you're in such a state that you have to ask somebody what won the race. All things are possible. But that's when the bookie really begins to love you. That's when he pays out, if not exactly with a smile, at least without a scowl. Because that's when he knows, beyond doubt, that you'll give it all back very quickly, and a lot more besides.

The odds are never in your favour. Sober, you may have a fighting chance by evaluating the odds and the stake-money. Not sober, you give no thought for tomorrow, and that should stand as an epitaph for every gambler who likes to flit back and foward, on a Saturday afternoon, from the pub to the betting-shop.

Not that I confined my gambling interests to race-horses. Dear me, no. If it was a bet, it was a bet, and I would stand for it.

In order to add just a touch of lighter news to this confession, if that's the word, let me talk about pool for a minute. Pool, in this case, being the cut-down, American-style form of snooker, and a game requiring fine skill. I was good at pool.

My pub was doing excellent business before Scotland passed laws which meant, in essence, all-day licensing, and we had to do something in the afternoons, between half-past-two and five o'clock. What we usually did was

Double-act with Davie Provan – a good man to have on your side, and Rangers-daft

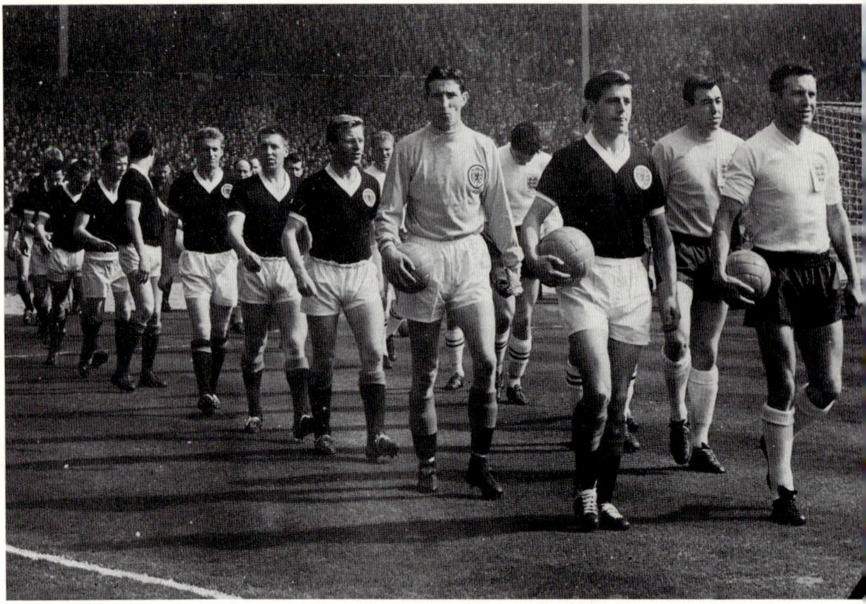

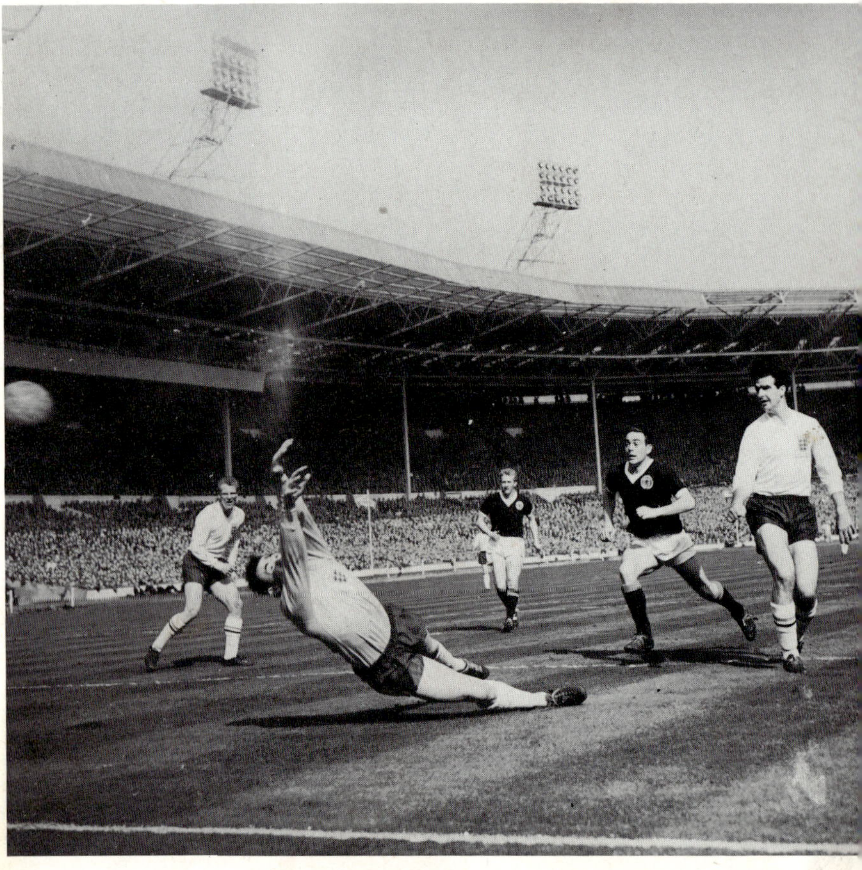

Above: Here you can see who scored. Yours truly, penalty kick, second goal, Wembley, 1963

Right: Denis Law, not the worst of goal-scorers, congratulates me on the penalty. Congratulations accepted with all due modesty

FACING PAGE:
Top: Here we go, against England in 1963, led out by Eric Caldow. That's me, sixth from the right, talking too much as usual

Bottom: You can't see me in this picture from Wembley, 1963. Never mind, it's a Baxter goal – and if Gordon Banks had stopped it, see how Ian St. John was waiting for the rebound

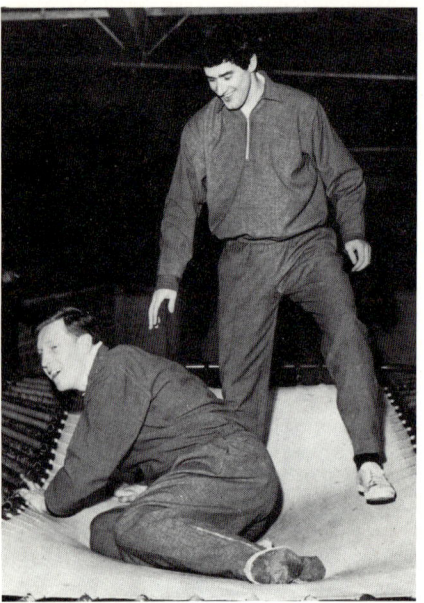

Billy McNeill is more dignified now, of course, and I'm sure, as always, a great guy. But he was never any use on the trampoline

Now isn't this a lovely picture! A collector's piece, I'd say. I'm actually controlling the ball with my right foot!

'I never touched him!' That's what I seem to be saying. I'm probably lying – we were playing England, after all

He was a cobra in the penalty area, an exceptional player and a good friend. Who else but Ralph Brand

play pool, for real money. It was a long way from tossing pennies behind the Fife slag-heaps, but the general principle was similar. Two people playing, betting against each other, and with substantial side-bets. It was commonplace to have side-bets of £100 a time, and I refer to a decade ago.

One day Willie Henderson, who had just been out in Hong Kong, called me at the pub, almost on closing-time – the official closing-time, that is, for those who were interested only in bevy. Could he come round for a bottle of lager, he asked, and could he bring George Mulholland with him? Big George Mulholland, I must explain, was not so much a Rangers supporter as a Rangers fanatic. He was, and doubtless still is, one of that happy breed content to pay to get into Ibrox and watch the grass grow. Half of the year he spent working on Canadian construction sites, the other half watching Rangers and Scotland back home. Quite a character, George.

I told Willie he was welcome to come round for lager, and that he could bring anybody he liked, especially George. So over he comes, the wee barra, as the Glasgow term has it, and he is his usual cheeky self. He sees that we are playing pool, and there's a right good few shillings floating about. The company consisted mainly of publicans and, as is well known, publicans do tend to spend well.

'Any chance of a game?' asks Willie.

'Certainly,' I say.

Now in that company, there was a very good friend of mine called Alex MacFarlane, a smooth lad, a natty dresser, but somebody you could rely on. Also he could play pool a little bit better than Paul Newman, and nobody ever tried to break his thumbs.

Willie had met Alex previously, and, for some reason, didn't like him. It could have been because Alex did always look smart, while Willie – no matter how much his gear cost – was never likely to make the top ten in the list of best-dressed men. With Willie's figure, he might have been hard pressed to make the worst-dressed.

'Who do you want to play?' I asked Willie.

'Him,' said Willie, nodding to Alex. 'Twenty-five quid, is that all right?'

Alex, whom Willie had never seen play, placidly agreed, wondering, I suspect, where his next Santa Claus was coming from. Alex broke and nothing went in. Willie took over, and he must have potted five in a row. He was laughing his head off.

'Stanley,' he said to me, 'get some cold water, and pour it over this cue. It's red hot, I can hardly hold it. I'm just too good.'

Bets were now being struck all around the room, and nobody who knew anything was putting a penny on Willie. I'm not sure how much Willie was losing by five o'clock, but it couldn't have been less than £600. He hadn't really been set up. He had set himself up. Big Mulholland was tired from cashing travellers' cheques for him, because Willie just refused to give in. He thought he was unlucky, that's all. Eventually, we took the view that we had kept Willie on the table long enough. Apart from that, the travellers' cheques had run out.

'I'll need to go home now,' said Willie, 'but I'll tell you something, that was the dearest bottle of lager I've ever had.' Then he turned to Alex, and he was not looking pleased. 'You, sir, I'll be back tomorrow, for my money back, all right?'

'That's certainly all right,' said Alex. 'But listen, wee man, is it a promise? Because if it is, I'll send a Rolls Royce round for you.'

That was one of the better memories of gambling, and it was gambling which really got me in trouble, no question of that. It's not so long ago that I had £20,000 in my back pocket, not a debt in the world, and earning plenty from the pub. But I managed to blow it all.

The shoot-pontoon games were cruel, and if you know shoot-pontoon, you may understand why. One of my customers threw the keys of his Mercedes into the pot, covering more than £4000, and he got a taxi home.

One afternoon, in the lounge of the pub, I drew an RAF-style circle on the carpet, and played this two-handicap lad from Bearsden at putting – so many points per circle, top points for the bull. By opening time at five o'clock, I was £600 down, and when one of the barmaids came through and asked me to open the lounge, I wasn't too happy with her. 'Hell with the lounge,' I said, 'I've got to get some of this back.'

Fortified by Bacardi, I was growing more and more confident, or I thought I was. Luckily, my opponent was also drinking well, and he was definitely not improving. It reached the stage, at about nine o'clock, when he could hardly draw the club-head back. Nor could I, come to that. But I was £200 to the good, plus his cheque for £500, which was a lot better than opening the lounge. Next morning, he was round to claim the cheque for cash.

'You fancy a large Bacardi?' I asked him. I felt it was the least I could do. He did not appreciate the gesture.

'You,' he said, 'I'll never be in your bloody pub again.'

'Well, that's charming,' I said, 'that's not what you were saying at six o'clock last night, when you were busy stealing all my poppy.'

I've never seen him since, and I don't suppose that bothers him either.

Damon Runyan would surely have been in his element, writing about some of the characters who frequented the pub. What, I wonder, would he have called Big Tam, who used to play the horses with me on Saturday afternoons, by far the most dangerous time of the week. That's when animals with three legs come home out of the blue – putting you into the red – at 50–1. It's when course stewards turn a blind eye to strokes which, if pulled anywhere else, would mean jail.

Once we began with £40 each, choosing a horse in

turn. After five races, we were £400 down between us, and, at the sixth attempt, Tam said, 'What'll it be this time, then?' and he wasn't asking what I would like to drink.

I was now getting very irritated. 'You back what you like,' I said. 'Just leave me out of it. You're a bloody jinx.'

He went into the sulks for a minute or so, but quickly brightened up. I knew what was going through his mind. This time, he was thinking, he would be lucky.

Now had there been any justice, that would indeed have been Tam's lucky one. It was favourite, and it lost to a 10–1 shot. Guess who backed the winner, £150 single. Tam's normal good nature snapped. Looking round for something to hit me with, he found one of those Churchill-size cigars, the ones that come in long wooden coffins. I was still laughing when he hit me so hard across the head with it that it broke. I wouldn't have minded so much, but the cigar was unsmokeable.

It was wee George who invented the game of 'Shoes'. We would take turns in being the bookie, and bet with the company on what kind of shoes, or what colour, would be worn by the next person to walk into the public bar. Black or brown shoes would be joint favourites at even-money, and the odds would rise to 10–1 for wellington boots. George loved to be the bookie. Why, I'll never know. I never knew any other bookie who always lost.

After years of bad luck, at everything from horses to cards to casinos, George decided to emigrate to Canada. It was quite a sentimental moment in the pub on his last night. As he was about to leave, feeling no pain, he came up to me. 'Jim,' he said, and this is God's honest truth, 'I'd like you to have this, for old time's sake.' He handed me a little wallet. 'It's my membership card for the Chevalier Casino,' he explained. 'And it's got my lucky penny inside it.' I still have George's lucky penny, but I keep it under the bed. It seems to make more sense, there.

On another occasion, a very hard gentleman, whom I will not name for reasons of health, had been drinking all day in my pub and losing plenty at the 'tossing'. To be honest, he was one of the better ones, for all his hardness. Strangely it often happens that way – the tougher the man, the more pleasant the nature. But it's not easy to feel all at ease with the world when you're about £2,000 down and on your second bottle. This hard nut decided he would go to the toilet, which was upstairs. A minute later, I too felt that this might be a good idea. I found him piddling away, quite happily, in the hallway.

I don't know where I got the 'bottle' from – maybe from Bacardi? – because we are talking about six-foot-two of bone and muscle plus a mentality that didn't have much regard for consequences. But I remonstrated with him, shall we say, and when he told me what to do, I jumped on his back. That was a bad idea. He threw me, oh, about ten feet away into the nearest corner. Then he disappeared into the bar, and came back with a full lemonade bottle. This, I said to myself, is it. You're not going to wriggle your way out of this one.

He looked down at me. 'Sorry, Jim,' he said. 'I was out of order. But I'll tell you what I'll do. Hit me with this bottle, and we'll call it square, okay?' Well, what could I do, but grasp not the bottle but the metaphorical olive branch, and adjourn to the bar, where we bought each other more drinks?

On the whole, however, it wasn't the gambling in the pub that caught up with me in the end. There, at least, the odds were fair, whether we were playing at cards, pool or two-up. Horses and casinos – they were different. The bookmaker and the house always has an in-built advantage, and anyone who gambles big and consistently is going to lose in the end. My apologies if I have made this point before. Believe me, it is worth emphasizing.

At Sunderland, the casinos were particularly unlucky for me, perhaps because I was earning more than when at Ibrox, and so gambled more.

And once, when I was with Nottingham Forest, I went to York races with a couple of other Forest players, and won just over £5,500. We should have gone back to Nottingham that evening, for training in the morning. Instead – for it was a two-day meeting – we stayed the night in York, made feeble excuses to the club, and went back to the races. There my £5,500 vanished, and a good bit more besides.

There's a saying that all gamblers are either greedy or needy. I was in the greedy category. But the thrill was still there, and small bets were no use. I had to bet enough to feel sore when I lost. And whatever I won, it was never quite enough. Ian St. John would probably testify to that. With the Scotland squad at Largs, I was sharing a room with Ian, and he will remember how I showed him a hold-all stuffed with about £3,000 in readies. I had just won it, in a Glasgow casino. After the match in the evening, I was back at the casino. In the morning, I was broke.

So it's not easy to estimate how much I have lost, gambling, since 1960, when I first arrived at Ibrox, a skinny, fresh-faced wee boy from Fife. But if I relate it to what I have earned, and do some fairly basic calculations, I would say not less than £200,000. That's not money just gambled, not stake-money. It's money actually lost. So it's not in the Sir Hugh Fraser class, but it's a damned good try.

Other things, of course, contributed to my financial decline. My pub in Paisley Road West – I had it for 13 years – was a great business for at least five years, but then they started knocking down many of the houses in the area. Also, no small point, Rangers were playing rubbish, which meant that fewer and fewer fans were going to Ibrox – and calling in for a half at Jim Baxter's on the way.

But the pub could have been built up again, if I had had the inclination, and Rangers were always due for some sort of revival. That's why I'm not crying. I've always tried to be honest with myself. In that vein, I've only one question. Where's the next party, lads?